PENGUIN COMPASS

THE INTUITIVE WRITER

GAIL SHER'S expertise crosses several disciplines. She was named Teacher of the Year by the combined Education Faculties of Unversity of California at Berkeley, Stanford, and San Francisco State University and has taught classes in writing, psychology, and Zen at the graduate level for many years. Sher currently leads workshops nationwide, and facilitates writing groups in the Bay Area using the practices developed in this book and in *One Continuous Mistake: Four Noble Truths for Writers* (Penguin, 1999).

Sher is also an accomplished poet, the author of four book-length haiku sequences and eight books of avant-garde poetry. Her work has appeared in more than twenty literary journals, and her haiku have won awards in both the United States and Japan. Her first published book, *From a Baker's Kitchen* (1984), was based on her work as the founding baker of the now-famous Tassajara Bread Bakery. Sher is one of just ninety-six people to be ordained as a Zen monk by Shunryu Suzuki, the man credited with bringing Soto Zen practice to the West. She recently completed a spiritual autobiography based on her experiences at Tassajara Zen Monastery, called *Moon of the Swaying Buds*.

As a psychotherapist and as a coach, Sher supervises and consults with individuals and couples. She specializes in work with w͟r͟i͟t͟e͟r͟s. For further infor-mation or to c͟o͟n͟t͟a͟c͟t her, visit her website, www.gailsher.c͟o͟m.

THE

INTUITIVE WRITER

LISTENING TO YOUR OWN VOICE

GAIL SHER

PENGUIN
COMPASS

PENGUIN COMPASS

Published by the Penguin Group
Penguin Putnam Inc., 375 Hudson Street,
New York, New York 10014, U.S.A.
Penguin Books Ltd, 80 Strand, London WC2R 0RL, England
Penguin Books Australia Ltd, 250 Camberwell Road, Camberwell,
Victoria 3124, Australia
Penguin Books Canada Ltd, 10 Alcorn Avenue,
Toronto, Ontario, Canada M4V 3B2
Penguin Books India (P) Ltd, 11 Community Centre, Panchsheel Park,
New Delhi—110 017, India
Penguin Books (N.Z.) Ltd, Cnr Rosedale and Airborne Roads, Albany,
Auckland, New Zealand
Penguin Books (South Africa) (Pty) Ltd, 24 Sturdee Avenue,
Rosebank, Johannesburg 2196, South Africa

Penguin Books Ltd, Registered Offices:
Harmondsworth, Middlesex, England

First published in Penguin Compass 2002

1 3 5 7 9 10 8 6 4 2

Library of Congress Cataloging in Publication Data
Sher, Gail, 1942–
The intuitive writer : listening to your own voice / Gail Sher.
p.   cm.
Includes bibliographical references.
ISBN 0-14-219604-5 (pbk.)
1. Authorship.   I. Title.

PN145 .S458 2002
808'.02—dc21   2001036776

Printed in the United States of America
Set in Bulmer and Futura
Designed by M. Paul

For Brendan

TABLE OF CONTENTS

LISTENING TO WORDS

PROCESS

LISTENING IS FOREVER; AN APOTHEOSIS

ACKNOWLEDGMENTS

But to have gathered from the air a live tradition

or from a fine old eye the unconquered flame

This is not vanity.

Here error is all in the not done,

all in the diffidence that faltered . . .

—*Ezra Pound*, Cantos

First is letter prose-writer Merry White Benezra who swims through language (and its dross) like a sylph. I remain her indebted student.

When my agent Sarah Jane Freymann said, "Hey Gail. Reading your book aroused in me the very quality of listening . . . ," I almost cried. Thank you so much. (It's called poetry.)

My editor Carole DeSanti's allegiance, along with the endless invisible supportive practices of my assistants Lis Jorgens and Judi Clark rest in my heart, consoling and inspiring me.

To my Zen teacher, Shunryu Suzuki-roshi, and my guru, Paramahansa Yogananda, I bow with infinite gratitude.

THE
INTUITIVE WRITER

INTRODUCTION

THE STONE WOMAN
GIVING BIRTH

MONK: "Where can I enter Zen?"

MASTER GENSHA: "Can you hear the babbling brook?"

MONK: "Yes, I can hear it."

MASTER GENSHA: "Then enter there."[1]

In ancient Japan, if you wanted to study a martial art, you sought out a master and asked to become his student. When he accepted you, your training began. After any number of years, the master might say, "You're ready now. Teach on your own." At that point, your training was over.

At the beginning of your training, you would be given a white belt to hold your *gi* together. After much time, the white belt, which musn't be washed, would get extremely dirty. Eventually it became so stained that it could only be called a black belt. By some indiscernible process, you gradually became the black belt along with your uniform.

Learning without a reference point, while in vogue in

the East, is problematic for Westerners, who generally want to know where they stand. "How am I doing?" they ask, a question that rivets around "I." "How" is not important (usually) and "doing" has only one correlative—BEST! (in comparison to everyone else). "BEST" is the measurement of the value of "I" that often allows "me" to continue existing.

What's missing from this picture? One answer is *joriki* (the power of concentration). It releases the "I" that exists-because-it-exists-because-it-exists.

Joriki builds up slowly, non-linearly. Skipping steps equals going backward. Skipping steps leads to pride, and pride leads to (a sense of) expertise. Expertise leaves no gaps, no questions, no quest. Death.

The imagining ear picks up (hears) one's question and, by bringing it into sharp focus, transmutes it into doubt. Doubt leads to an entry point—an entry to a Way. Writers, by doubt, enter the "Way" of writing.

OUR WAY IS TO PRAISE AND ACCEPT EVERYTHING

———

What is the difference between imagination and the imagining ear?

Delightful though it may be, imagination can be a form of dissociation. If one is in pain, one might pretend not to be. If one is bored, one may inwardly soar to a celestial world. Imagination will fly us anywhere. Exploring one's imagination is like exploring the outer reaches of one's exquisitely pleasure-saturated potential self.

The imagining ear, on the other hand, is grounded in the present. It is right here, right now. While it may feel muddy, dirty, wet . . . buried at the bottom is a different kind of pleasure—freedom.

Bikers, junkies, burglars, thieves—they thrash around one's heart of hearts. Their pain. Their suffering. (Innocence is not-to-touch.)

Including the imagination. Don't even picture your body more narrow, your mind more agile, your soul more stout. Don't go there. Don't go anywhere. Simply stay where you are.

Turn on your imagining ear and tune in to your ignorant fat fragility. Have a chat. Talk long into the night. Allow the situation to purify the situation.

The more company you keep it, the more power you'll assume. Pretty soon it (the situation) will be powerless without you. You may not have control, but you'll have your friendly life.

Listening closely to your imagining ear, you'll hear your self-disdain. But you can't whip it into silence or kick it out. *Hearing* it out, however, *is* an option.

"What is being asked of me?" equals the imagining ear's mantra. "What shall my offering be, here, right now?" The secret (*magikos* for a writer) is that the imagining ear doesn't need imagination to liberate suffering from the (internal or external) world.

LISTENING
TO ONESELF

I am always tuning my orchestra. Somewhere deep inside there is a sound that is mine alone, and I struggle daily to hear it and tune my life to it. Sometimes there are people and situations that help me to hear my note more clearly; other times, people and situations make it harder for me to hear. A lot depends on my commitment to listening and my intention to stay coherent with this note. It is only when my life is tuned to my note that I can play life's mysterious and holy music without tainting it with my own discordance, my own bitterness, resentment, agendas, and fears.

—*Rachel Naomi Remen*[2]

The imagining ear's intrinsic energy has four qualities. The first is peace. Peace feels gentle, pure, expansive, but also fresh and quick.

When we begin a work of art, a certain drive develops. Inside one is on fire, but it is a "fire of peace," reflected in the mind as openness and in the body as an absence of speed.

The sacred is still, not lazy. It faces its demons head-on. In the presence of truth, compassion arises. And with compassion, peace (and its concomitant grace).

The second is richness, which includes joy. Think of a room, lovingly arranged by you so that at your fingertips is everything you need for your writing.

Joy is luscious, spacious, open. Which is not a prescription. Jewish-mother spreads are plentiful-luscious. Japanese rooms are spare-luscious. Neither feature scarcity.

The third is basic goodness, which includes the notions of generosity, bravery, confidence. Once there is richness (no poverty), we can let go, meet the minds of others.

The fourth is harmony plus inquisitiveness. Its nature is fearless. A writer's path involves congruity, mellifluousness, speculation, perseverence. Untouched by ambition or pain.

Realizing peace, richness, basic goodness, and harmony plus inquisitiveness, one's hearing becomes balanced. Neither accepting too eagerly nor rejecting too violently, we simply rest in the imagining ear's steady drive.

TWELVE MARKS OF THE IMAGINING EAR

For a writer, developing an imagining ear is the work of a lifetime. It involves deepening her relationship with herself and everything that crosses her path. Enhanced by non-doing, anonymity, self-sacrifice, ultimately it is about her awareness of the world—her commitment to hearing it day after day with a beginner's mind.

A beginner's mind is not about erasing anything or pretending not to know something. Judgment inhibits a beginner's mind. We can know a lot and still preserve a beginner's mind if our basic stance is curious. "Expertise" simply means being expert at discovering (discerning) increasingly infinitesimal (almost unhearable) parts of oneself and one's reality.

We don't need to understand. Feelings, like food, are digested, not justified. We garner the creative impulse they provide and slough off the rest.

Something unheard is outgrown. We strain our ears to attend the yet more subtle. Allowing, nourishing, and cultivating the disappearing echoes in our bodies, mind, and heart are how the imagining ear thrives.

A listening-pilgrim's progress is gauged not so much by location as by humility, alertness, gratitude. Remembering who we are (handling words with respect) together, we, as writers, realize ourselves, by spiraling through the imagining ear's twelve marks:

> non-aggression
> creating gaps
> surrender
> compassion
> favoring the ineffable
> precision detail
> rapt attention
> non-discrimination
> bowing
> composure, grace, and decorum
> austerity
> authenticity

DHARMA ART

Chogyam Trungpa Rinpoche coined the term "*dharma art.*"[3] "*Dharma*" means "norm" or "truth." In the context of art, it refers to the state before one performs any action.

If you are a writer, you are a writer always, not just while you are writing. Your imagining ear is turned on twenty-four hours a day.

Writers listen slowly. They listen inward, outward, then around the world in the four directions.

Each thing heard blasts off freely (without constraint, without expectation, without manipulation or play). When astral me hears astral you, the pipeline is pure. This is the beginning of writing.

"I" start by erasing myself. The imagining ear kicks in, abiding in the way I do things.

Sometimes we try to take advantage of our world, to milk it or slaughter it. Consider our attitude toward cows.

If they don't produce anything (or if it looks like they won't), we slit their throats and eat them up. *That's* aggression.

LISTENING SLOWLY (I)

It is said in Java that the tiger's hearing is so acute that hunters must keep their nose hairs cut lest the tiger hear their breath whistle through their nostrils; it is also known that the tiger's strength is supernatural.

—*Peter Matthiessen*[4]

Right listening does not mean "right" as opposed to "wrong." It means "right" in the sense of comprehensive or complete. It arises from wholeness, from willingness (enthusiasm) to be who we are.

When the Zulus of South Africa speak English, they polish and smooth every syllable. Words slow down, become something else. "Okay" and "yes" equal "okaaaay," "yehezz." "Izzz it?," which could mean "Is that a fact?," follows "I'm getting hungry."

Rich, melodious, patient, their English absorbs, expanding their capacity for experiencing pain.

Writers sit upright in a ring of pain. They feel it, ache with it. They are built to ache with it, like a yogi is built to relax and breathe—slowly, in and out.

LISTENING SLOWLY (II)

> It seemed as if we could hear the corn growing in the
> night; under the stars one caught a faint crackling in the
> dewy, heavy-odoured cornfields where the feathered
> stalks stood so juicy and green.
>
> —*Willa Cather*[5]

For writers, listening is a form of solace (it can cure spiritual, emotional, and psychological agony).

Usually we are restless. We hear something and jump to some thought—either about what it is or what it means we have to do about it. Just listening makes us shy.

But shyness can also be a kind of aggression. If we hear something extremely beautiful, we become so fascinated (intrigued), we end up hearing mostly our desire, which yearns to consume that thing.

Silence can be scary. To hear one's heart, one must

feel safe. It takes a certain amount of leisure to allow oneself the space (receptivity) to simply hear and rest in hearing.

LISTENING SLOWLY (III)

Hearing is also a kind of sacrament. Through *this* body, through *these* ears, the entire universe is able to hear itself.

If you seek hearing elsewhere, even though hearing is everywhere, you will not hear because your hearing is not consummated. (Even though you practice, it is only a ritual that you practice.)

To purify our hearing we must give it away. Anything that is given is purified by the act of giving, provided the giving is "pure." (Purity is determined by its origins—prior to behavior.)

Each has a proclivity toward a special variety. Some sweep leaves. Some study texts. Some boil rice. Some simply listen to the whirling wind. The question is not *what*. It is *how intently*. If you listen slowly, with an open heart, you will transmute pain into compassion (the psychic stance of good writing) and become who you are as a writer.

[c r e a t i n g   g a p s]

The imagining ear creates a vacuum surrounding each hearing event. It creates gaps for pure hearing to be.

A gap allows for essential me. (Anything produced without a gap or pause beforehand is by definition aggressive.)

We need space to balance our fears so that we can hear them with our imagining ear. Without this space (a big wide gap to move around, stretch, figure things out), whatever we fear will show up in our writing as a blind spot.

FORM BRED IN THE BONE

[creating gaps]

—

Stravinsky's *Violin Concerto* is as much about silence as sound, musician Richard Sennett remarks. About Balanchine's choreography he says, "The dance builds on musical absence."[6]

"Watching silence" thus becomes Sennett's obsession. He nightly attends the ballet in order to understand music he himself performs elsewhere.

Balanchine insisted his dances are just dances: "You will never find any literary meaning in my dance." (Unlike ballet, every gesture in modern dance has a literary meaning is his implication.)

If Sennett is seeking to understand music by "watching music," why then ballet?

"You think you want modern dance—I'll give you antiballet," said Balanchine, who made "grammars of movement." "Second sight" (his equivalent to the photographer's) is not about "seeing" but about "being there."[7]

The imagining ear too makes grammars of movement, disappearing rules, and second "sounds" primarily about "presence."

Writing what you've heard (like a jazz musician a tune) involves first "hearing absence" (the possibilities of the un-said), then making a grammar of non-sound.

CHILD'S POSE

In yoga, the child's pose, which requires discovering one's breath when one's lungs are restricted, arouses a subtle kind of strength. One must relax, surrender to the posture, and gradually find (reconnect with) one's breathing.

While surrender takes a will of steel, when surrender is called for, it is wise to abide. Faking is useless. You can't anyway because the body doesn't lie.

Aggression prevents surrender. (Aggression is the opposite of being malleable, trusting, becoming larger by becoming smaller, more powerful via vulnerability.)

Surrender means listening with your heart (not your head). It says "yes" to the supplicant, votes for the other side, slows down at the finish line. Surrender, when authentic, is unpredictable. It just shows up (it doesn't hide).

If you try to get rid of your aggression, you may distract yourself from facing it. Give yourself to it instead.

Your imagining ear will suffuse it with love—the real tool a writer needs to yield (disappear), absorb the suffering of her subject.

I'M A WRITER. WRITERS WRITE. IN A LOYAL CONSCIOUSNESS THE IMAGINING EAR FLOURISHES.

[surrender]

In 1932, painter Harlen Hubbard, whose main subject was the Ohio River Valley, sent a portrait of his mother to a juryless exhibition at the Cincinnati Art Museum. When he traveled to see the show, he found it hanging in the obscurest corner of the tiniest room. He wrote,

> *I do not understand why anyone who has painted as long and seriously as I have, and who has asked so little, should have absolutely no success or recognition. But I have gone this far and now I must go on.*[8]

By 1936, his defiance had, as Wendell Berry put it, "achieved a kind of style: 'I will paint for myself and turn the canvases to the wall.'"

By 1941, Hubbard was saying,

I come alone to this task of painting. No one wants the pictures or understands or encourages their production. I feel so strongly that I must sever completely all possible connection with this world, and live on the outside fringe, a rebel.[9]

In the negativity of his rejecters, Hubbard found not only an affirmation of the painting itself, but also a recognition that his failure preserved his connection with the source of his work.

"No Paintings for Sale" Hubbard firmly tacked across the door of his studio when he realized that the mere hope of sales and acceptance by other artists had created a psychic trap.[10] Not until he could paint without even the possibility of selling, would he be able entirely to surrender to himself.

BIT PLAYERS

[c o m p a s s i o n]

———

I'm sorry but I can't eat this. I publish rabbits!

—*Ursula Nordstrom*[11]

The Old Testament tells the story of Joseph, whose eleven brothers detested his father's favorite. One day when the brothers were in a field tending the family flock, Jacob sent Joseph to find them. A stranger Joseph met pointed out the way.

"Bit players" are exceedingly rare in the Torah. Indeed, Rashi (a Talmud scholar) identifies this stranger as the Angel Gabriel. Gabriel embodies the principle that each being who crosses our path has something indispensable to teach us, though we may not realize (understand, or even get) that there has been a lesson until later.

This man averted the course of Joseph's life, the life of
his family, the history of his people, and the fate of that
whole part of the world at that time, because all these
things depended on what would happen to Joseph next,
and what would happen to Joseph next could not, in
fact, happen until he found his brothers in Dothan.[12]

Elijah the Prophet, hero of numerous Talmudic tales, is, according to legend, the only mortal who has ever left Earth without dying. He goes up to heaven in a chariot of fire and comes back down with important information. Throughout Jewish history, he appears in different places, in different guises, unrecognized and usually when people are desperate.

Since Elijah is always in disguise, anyone could be this harbinger of the messiah.

Our loss of reverence for self-listening has had a ripple effect. Writers (tuning instead to an empyreal editor's pitch) may not trouble themselves to develop it. On the bier of gossip, misinformation, self-violence (harsh judgment or criticism), and projection, we sacrifice our bit players, potentially Elijah, in the form of a creative thought.

BEING COMPLETELY WHO WE ARE, WE ENTER THE WORLD OF FERTILITY

[c o m p a s s i o n]

Huang T'ing-chien praised T'ao Yuan-ming by saying, "Yuan-ming did not make poems—he depicted the wonders that were in his heart, that was all."[13] *Su Tung-p'o (1037–1101) comments: "Only when you have reached a stage where you have forgotten about poetry can you begin to talk about poems." (Fires start in the heart.)*

"Poetry works not by describing its subject with detached objectivity from without, but by imaginatively entering inside its subject so as to disclose it from within," translator and Buddhist scholar Stephen Batchelor tells us.[14] To do so—to hear through silence—requires renunciation.

Renunciation is not something that we do. It is something that we realize. The gateway is intimacy, not just with humans and animals, but with all sentient beings, including ourselves.

If we are stingy with ourselves, we will not learn how or why things come to us and will not truly be able to give them away. Not only is everything that comes to us an opportunity to understand renunciation; everything that comes to us *is* renunciation. But we must hear how. Listening with our imagining ear to the part of us that knows how is how to learn how.

Holding back too much or letting go of too much functions like a lie. Not realizing who we are (and therefore what is appropriate for us) is a form of ignorance (ignoring the inner voice that tells us who we are). Wishing ourselves well and again wishing ourselves well (discovering what is ours so that it can be, via others, ours) is the way a writer develops love.

The reason to be focused (centered, present) when seeing or hearing is to erase the toxicity of time. The impact of time is minimized because the impact of karma is minimized. The purity (*Tao*) of an object seen (or word heard) is not defiled by the baggage of the viewer/listener. Its flow is unobstructed.

In the light of next morning, our kitchen window looked sorry for itself. Macaroni tubes had congealed on the panes in the night, the flowery sashed curtains were stained cheesy yellow. Our stepfather sat with his head in his hands over the toast and eggs our mother had fried in lard as usual, to soak up his hangover.

"What you goggling at?" He looked up, bloodshot, to catch Laurie, Sarah and me staring across the table while he lobbed salsa into his yolks. He tutted when our mother let a glass slip through her shaky fingers while

she was washing it, so that it splintered against the
tap. "Pathetic bloody cow: pull yourself together!" [15]

Skilled writers hear even when they're seeing, tasting, smelling, touching. Their ear is so developed they hear right through whatever sense into the heart of their character's matter.

God's menorah is of people, not of candles. When God says, "Let there be light," for a writer it means, sometimes we discover the place in us that carries light only after it has become dark.

There is a story in the Old Testament in which God says that he will allow the world to continue so long as there is a minimum of thirty-six beings capable of compassion in the midst of human suffering. These thirty-six are called the Lamed-Vov.

Only God knows who they are. Even they do not know the role they play in the continuation of the universe. They respond to suffering, not to save the world, but simply because it matters to them.

Because no one knows who they are, anyone could be one of them. Everyone we meet, including our self, must be heard (written) into the fullest possibility of life.

Listen, for example, to Andrea Ashworth:

Worry muscled and cramped in my calves, kneeling over the puzzles. I left my sisters and tiptoed back down the hall to my mother's door, where a sly twist of my kirby grip slid open the lock. Her face was buried under the blankets. I had to peel them slowly back, holding my heart down.

No splits or gashes. All the bones where they should be.

I let myself breathe. Around her eyes the skin puffed veiny blue with bursts of purple, then sagged, yellow-green and hollow, under the cheekbones. Her dimples were shadowy holes, carved deep into the cheeks.

I bent to kiss the smell of my mother's messed-up face. It was comforting, when her sores made her look a bit like a stranger, to find the same old scents. Woody perfume came from her hair, rich with hours of sipping coffee and huffing on cigarettes in her pink housecoat and green fur slippers.

"Andy, love?" Her eyeballs shifted under bluish skin lids.

I hovered—wake up, wake up, wake up—over the closed eyes.

My mother's head lolled in the damp pillow. I bent closer to catch her murmurs, before they faded and *slowed. She sank back into bruised sleep, and I let her be.*[16]

Its love Ashworth *hears.* She *hears* love and she *hears* with love, sidling up and *listening* closely.

When our mother was what she called recuperated, the door would creak open. The toilet flushed and gurgled. She flapped down the hall in her slippers to cook tea.[17]

Because she *hears,* we *hear*—the cheap wooden door, warped, bruised, chipped, squeaking slowly open as Andrea's mother, still in a daze from her husband's rampage, not at all recuperated (which belies the entrenched cyclical nature of the battering dynamic), tolling like a bell.

Because Ashworth *hears,* we *hear* that particular clakity gush whose vigor astonishes. There is one at the beach road inn, down the hallway at the bed and breakfast, and, thank God, in the filthy restroom at the gas station. All this previous *hearing* informs our *hearing* of Andrea's mother's toilet as it fails to flush away the promise of more and more and more bruises.

We *hear* Andrea's mother's slippers flippity flopping

down the passage, cavernous as it must feel inside Andrea's mother's smashed head. Maybe the floor is wood. Maybe scabby carpet whose once-rose floral design has long since faded into puke. Either way, there's no padding to absorb her wounds. Her daughter's heart is all.

MY WHITE AND YOUR WHITE AREN'T NECESSARILY THE SAME

Matisse told Picasso it was round about this time that he began to pay attention to the boldness and spontaneity of his children's artwork. Pierre copied his father's painting of a rose in a pottery jug brought back from Biskra. He also invented a new colour, and remembered all his life how crushed he felt when his father pointed out that there was no such thing.[18]

There is a basic iconographic pattern in the universe (the seasons, for example), but our relationship to it is our own. How we hear it is our own, and is therefore unpredictable. Magic is tailor-made personal power.

No one needs to confirm our experience, which is unconditional. We confirm it. The only magic that exists is personal, real, direct.

Your imagining ear, facilitating this enlightened expression, is also direct and personal. It resonates to the cumulative essence of your radiance, luminosity, emptiness. Everything that you do, say, dream, write contributes to its nature.

———

As dusk approaches in the hinterlands, a traveler pon-ders shelter for the night. He notices tall rushes grow-ing everywhere, so he bundles an armful together as they stand in the field, and knots them at the top. Presto, a living grass hut. The next morning, before embarking on another day's journey, he unknots the rushes and presto, the hut de-constructs, disappears, and becomes a virtually indistinguishable part of the larger field of rushes once again. The original wilder-ness seems to be restored, but minute traces of the shel-ter remain. A slight twist or bend in a reed here and there. There is also the memory of the hut in the mind of the traveler—and in the mind of the reader reading the description.[19]

This place of constant evolving and devolving, of imperfection, inconspicuousness (the hidden, tentative, ephemeral)—this is the locale of the imagining ear.

To hear it one pauses, lavishes attention on the evocative evanescent.

Beauty is a dynamic that occurs between oneself and something else. It pops up. The closer to non-existent, the more exquisite.

"Things," being movement, "get on." One minute they have much to say; the next, there's silence and empty space.

In Ayurveda, "joints" (places where things come together) are ruled by *vata* (air). Like wind, they're here and gone. What is the difference between simple and austere? Between careful and fussy? Between sober and boring? Between clean (unencumbered) and sterile? I know and then I don't.

Resplendent, bewitching, compelling—herein lies the invisible connective tissue that imagining ears haunt. The body, not language, is the repository of knowledge. The density of information contained within an object changes, as does human relatability. A writer, using her imagining ear, leans on the accumulated resources of the overlooked.

THE EAR IS
WORTH TEN EYES

———

"When in stillness, one listens with the heart," says the Chinese pictogram for listening attentively. Listening attentively is the writer's highest form of service.

A writer writes without allegiance. None is possible because truth flees at its moment of apprehension. Allegiance is to non-allegiance. The intensity of the imagining ear's response is all.

Therefore, the anthem of specificity. "If you don't know something specifically, you don't know it," said Frost, stooping to immerse himself more deeply into a fern.[20]

The Wheel of Life (the Buddhist iconographic one) is a chart of our ordinary human experiences. Laundry done, we realize that life *is* worth celebrating. Why? Because there is immense dignity stemming from immersion in small, seemingly insignificant details. Staying with them (the poignance of staying with them) is the heart of a writer's work.

—————

The central Jewish declaration of faith is not "I believe," but "Hear, O Israel." The focus is on the ears not the lips—on listening, not speaking.[21]

Once upon a time, Rabbi Alan Lew was awakened in the middle of the night by the family of a dying member of his congregation who needed a rabbi to witness her reciting the *Shem'a.*

The word *shem'a* means "listen." It is composed of three mother sounds: *shin,* the sound of cacophony; *mem,* the harmony of all sound (as in *om*); and *ayin,* the functional equivalent of *aleph,* the silence that contains all sound. (All other sounds are derived from these three fundamental sounds.) The prayer *"Shem'a,"* called the watchword of the Jewish faith, declares the oneness of all things.

Hear, O Israel: Yahweh our God is the one Yahweh. You shall love Yahweh your God with all your heart, with all your soul, with all your strength. Let these words be written on your heart. Repeat them to your children and say them over whether at rest in your house or walking abroad, at your lying down or at your rising. Bind them as a sign on your hand and on your forehead as an emblem; write them on the door posts of your house and on your gates. (Deuteronomy 6:4-9; 11:13-21)

"How do I *enter* the *Shem'a*?" a writer might legitimately ask.

The Bobover Chasidim is a Jewish sect famous for its wildly ecstatic dancing. But they don't just bop into wild ecstatic dancing. First they sing. When they are completely filled with words, they sing a *nigun,* a song without words. And when that song has filled every cell of their body (when they are so full of it that they just can't stand it anymore), *then* they get up and dance, explains the Bobover Rebbe.[22]

"ONE WILL BECOME AN ARTIST WHEN ONE KNOWS WHAT IS NEEDED TO MAKE ART"

[rapt attention]

Sensation libre. That's the most difficult ingredient. Persistence, willpower, repetitive-numbing work. Or urgent hard work. All (for writers) are correct.

Don't forget that one must only be oneself. But you will have to work at it![23]

Hoping to generate in his son his own passionate taste for work, Pissarro wrote, "[The main thing] is the will to get up early in the morning and run to work, to withdraw oneself in it, to create a whole world."

In Pissarro's work ethic the notion of holidays or, worse, entertainments is sheer absurdity. "Pissarro probably never took a holiday in his life," his biographer wrote.

"Whenever he traveled from his home and studio, it was because he was either house hunting, or visiting his relatives or his wife's." Even then, the main thing was what he chanced upon to paint.

His letters to his son bespeak of his ardor, as well as the strenuousness of its physical and mental demands. But self-discipline and determination directly lead to liberty. Plain hard work brings freedom.

When you feel a certain thing, you have to do it at whatever cost. . . . It is so rare to want to do something that you really have to do it; you must even hurry, for it will just go away if you wait . . . now, go on. Believe me. Go on! . . . It is also the most practical thing to do!

Pissarro is described by Cézanne as an *acharne*, someone who is possessed by a need, who literally has it in his flesh. "Until the [Franco-Prussian] war, as you know, I lived in a mess," Cézanne wrote. "I wasted my whole life. When I think about it, it was only at L'Estaque that I came to fully understand Pissarro—painter, like myself—a workaholic. An obsessive love of work took hold of me."[24]

[n o n - d i s c r i m i n a t i o n]

Despite its reputation for descending in spurts, unannounced, in ill-begotten flashes, genuine inspiration is very ordinary.

Actually, becoming inspired is not something that you do. Through patience and self-compassion, it is something that you allow to happen.

It comes from settling down and accepting your blankness, which is not shameful. Inspiration is the continuous, interdependent, co-arising ground of your being, that your imagining ear (in the name of writing practice) first condenses then replicates.

> *. . . art is a by-product of the experience of being with yourself, of living within patience.*[25]

If you work alone for eighteen hours a day, you explore your mind for eighteen hours a day, says illustrator/

thangka painter Robert Beer. This exploration transforms your mind and in turn the artistic image that you produce. The important point is abiding within yourself. "Just to remain in that space and to let things arise and fade without having to grasp at them makes one realize that everything is already here, that no higher teaching is needed."

Our enemies are not stupidity, lack of talent, dullness (though these may be their facades). Hesitation and disinterest are the true obstacles to clearly hearing ourselves and our world.

FLOWER KIRTAN

When we first hear something, we are unsure. Is that something? Is it worthwhile? Before we hear, we have an inkling toward something. If we trust, remain open, mindful, upright, our inkling becomes a guide.

Our instinct toward wholeness has no genetic code. It's larger than body, mind, death, birth. An acorn houses the soul of an oak. If it is gobbled by a squirrel, it gets swallowed, digested, eliminated. But it doesn't lose its oak nature.

If we like red better than yellow, we may fail to find the beauty in yellow. That doesn't diminish yellow. We may be diminished by our inability to hear its lightness, but in the end, to feel whole—and to *write* from wholeness—we have to include everything.

THE SITUATION PURIFIES
THE SITUATION

[b o w i n g]

———

Writing is a ceremony. Ceremonies are meaning contain-ers. Bowing, bringing my conduct and intention into perfect accord—"I will write every day, no matter what"—actually means not doing anything at all.

Not-doing means being fully congruent with myself. (How is writing not-doing?)

When Marlon Brando was in acting school (so the story goes), his teacher said, "Imagine you're a chicken roosting in your coop when an atom bomb explodes." Brando simply sat. He was able to imagine "no imagina-tion"—not being able to imagine doing anything else.

Brando used the situation to purify the situation.

Writers constantly sit with "atom bombs" exploding. Befuddled or exasperated with the mires we create, we rack our brains for a better way to be.

Whirling ever faster in an exasperated vortex only

gets us deeper in the exasperated vortex. Accepting our situation (bowing)—ignoble, dumb, or silly though it may be—alertly resting in its silliness—everything feels more friendly.

—

Years later I would come to know that the body has a vegetable mind, like a plant. It has its own agenda and intent, separate from the mind, the heart, the Will, and if you want to go your own way in spite of the body some negotiation is necessary.[26]

Wisdom, as anyone looking at a picture of His Holiness the Dalai Lama at age three instantly gets, shows in our eyes. Composure, grace, and decorum show in our posture. Qualities of mind manifest in the body, litmus test of one's understanding.

Qualities of mind, qualities of anything, however evanid, exist. We simply recognize them (given a modicum of education, training, and experience).

Integrity is the key to immersion in one's world. Integrity equals composure, grace, and decorum, all of which are attitudes. Composure is an attitude of stateliness and inner balance. Grace is non-aggressive, flexible, uplifted, cheerful. Decorum is gentle and kind, compassionate and open. Together they comprise presence.

The imagining ear hears with taste, which is a refined sense of the correctness of things. Taste is not based on monetary value. A rag can be correct or incorrect, based on its inherent nature.

> *... occasionally one sees something fleeting in the land, a moment when line, color, and movement intensify and something sacred is revealed, leading one to believe that there is another realm of reality corresponding to the physical one but different ... the land ... is inexplicably coherent, it is transcendent in its meaning, and it has the power to elevate a consideration of human life.*[27]

First there is ordinary hearing. Settling into the hearing, amalgamating oneself within one's hearing, arouses the imagining ear, which hears intentions, willpower, spirit, *prana, chi, shakti*—sounds unavailable to the ordinary ear. It's abrupt. It cuts through thoughts. With composure, grace, and decorum, the imagining ear perceives (and helps a writer integrate) a level of reality mysteriously hidden from her everyday (frantic) mind.

CONCENTRATED INSTANCES

[composure, grace, and decorum]

. . . Canadian woodchoppers [make their own] axe-handles, following the curve of the grain. . . . Art should follow lines in nature, like the grain of an axe-handle.

—Robert Frost[28]

"Lines in nature" also exist in me. The "curve of the grain" of my authentic voice speaks with presence and authority.

It's not a matter of finding the right path, but of finding one's own path. Matisse claimed that he discovered his artistic identity by looking through his early work and tracing something constant—a "sign of my personality, which came out the same no matter what different moods I passed through."[29]

". . . style in prose or verse is that which indicates how the writer *takes* himself and what he is saying," agreed Frost.[30]

Painter Fairfield Porter noted that after each annual exhibition, he could paint in the manner of skill he acquired during the spurt of effort that peaked at the exhibition, but no one is deceived.

And so I have to learn painting all over again, not to acquire skill again, but to acquire integrity, which is, after all, perhaps the only true skill.[31]

Integrity thrives in concentrated instances. An apple, a book, a flower are some. The writer's task is to hear them into life using words instead of oils. A word (or group of them) is a "thing" of daily life holding infinity, just like any other.

The anarchically personal, the radically autobiographical, the atheism of "idea in the absence of idea" all celebrate the metaphysical in Tuesday's leftovers. Hearing an object reduces it to its essence—thus to a form of style.

Nabokov was right. Style alone constitutes a writer's biography.

THE INVISIBLE PLENTITUDE
OF THE WORLD

[austerity]

The invisible plentitude of the world. Painters paint it. Singers sing it. Dancers dance it. What is their secret?

Runners refer to the "zone"—being "in the zone" as a coveted state of mind. Here, pain is superceded by pleasure—matter, mind. Beyond body, know-how, effort, and resistance, a calm descends and buoys one along as if she were a weightless wind.

People have different capacities for "the zone." Some slip into it quickly. Running is hard, but the payoff is count-on-ably forthcoming. Some achieve it with concerted effort. Some, no matter how much they try, are conditioned to experience it, at best, rarely. *You* tell *me* why.

Those in the third group can still become runners. They may even derive *more* satisfaction from their accomplishments. Rarely blissed out, they are present each moment for the full force of the pain.

The imagining ear is the writer's "zone." We try and try. Suddenly the writing writes itself. Pissarro worked like a maniac. One day, he simply understood: nothing is colder than full sunlight in summertime.

"THE REDWOOD FLOOR
RETURNED A DIFFERENT
RHYTHM FOR EACH OF
OUR FOOTFALLS"

[a u s t e r i t y]

―――

"Ballet is NOW," declared George Balanchine shortly before he died. "I don't want my ballets preserved as museum pieces for people to go and laugh at what used to be."[32] In his old age, Balanchine reworked *Apollo*, a ballet nearly everyone thought was perfect. The beginning and end were cut. Stravinsky's music was cut. Nearly a third of the ballet simply vanished.

Balanchine subscribed to Stravinsky's credo: "In classical dancing, I see the triumph of studied conception over vagueness, of the rule over the arbitrary, of order over the haphazard." He sought to discover the inner logic of a form by experimenting with its rules rather than preserving them intact, following them religiously. Stravinsky called this love of form ballet's "aristocratic austerity."[33]

For example, Balanchine was enamoured of the photographs of George Platt Lynes who, instead of capturing actual performance steps, photographed the ambience of a dance, its "echo" or "perfume." "They are pure miniatures," he wrote, "while dance-films are always improvised or impoverished . . . [and they] contain something of the secret and seldom realized intention of choreography."[34]

"Ballet is NOW." Writing is NOW. Studied simplicity, inner logic, aristocratic austerity are arrived at obliquely, by happy chance, and through puzzlement.

IMMACULATE, IMMENSE, AND LUXURIOUSLY SPARSE

[authenticity]

———

"The space had a sea-swept look that spoke clarity," Elaine said of William de Kooning's loft the night she first laid eyes on it.[35] He cleaned it weekly, which took more than half a day. "An eggshell from the inside" is how John Cage described his own sixth-floor apartment.

But de Kooning's mother scolded him (a generic scold that cut to the core): "You always liked the part of music that isn't music."

De Kooning didn't paint "talk" *about* art. Cage didn't play "music" *about* silence. De Kooning's generous retort (not to his mother directly) equals "Just because you don't do anything, doesn't mean you've said something."

According to the *vajrayana* tradition, non-aggression is the basis of hearing reality. Arising from non-aggression is a sense of dignity (in Tibetan *ziji*, which includes the notion of authenticity or presence). Centered in our authentic self, we hear things as they are, simply and directly.

In 1948, Jackson Pollock became contemptuous at a party to Arshile Gorky's face:

"Gorky, they're [your paintings are] just weak . . . ," he whined. Gorky paused a moment and then, with a lethal smile, reaching slowly into his coat pocket, pulled out a large knife, and carefully opened it. He removed a pencil from another pocket and began to sharpen it with the precision of a Zen master, all the while keeping his eyes fastened on Jackson's face. Hypnotized, Jackson and everyone in the room watched in silence as the tip of the pencil came to a surgically sharp needle point, in what seemed a symbolic ritual. Gorky took a deep breath and blew solemnly on the point, which instantly shined. "Mr. Pollock," he cooed with mock affection, "you and I are different kinds of artists."[36]

(Had *you* been Gorky . . . ?)

"Nothing grows under big trees," de Kooning replied when asked why he never studied with a famous artist. His student pressed, "How does one become a famous artist?"

DE KOONING: "What are you painting?"

STUDENT: "I'm having a terrible time. All I seem to be making are bad paintings; the more I paint, the worse I get."

DE KOONING: "Don't tell anyone; they might steal your idea."[37]

"Instead of Edwin Denby writing about Markova's dancing, Markova should dance about Edwin's writing," de Kooning commented to his fellow artists one night at the Automat. [38]

Knowing absolutely that your ideas are unstealable is how one becomes a famous artist.

"...LIKE A BEACHED WHALE, SLOWLY DRYING UP"

[e x e r c i s e]

Language is the self, reflected and clothed in nouns and verbs and adjectives. Without Farsi, the Iranian in Mina [Gelareh Asayesh's young daughter] will shrivel up and die. Even as I think this, I know that my greatest fear is my own inner shriveling, not Mina's. In guarding Mina's heritage, I guard my own, for they are linked. My daughter, this piping voice in my house speaking the words I learned at my mother's knee, is a lifeline to my first self.

—*Gelareh Asayesh*[39]

Language *is* the self, reflected and clothed in nouns and verbs and adjectives. But clothing gets worn, mirrors scar and shatter. First, find a word that has perished (an "endangered species" word); then resuscitate it, using your writerly magic.

A COCKLESHELL APPROACH

We are all a product of our physical geography; it is as if the contours of earth and water and leaf that fill our eyes [ears] during childhood create a corresponding landscape of the mind. It lingers dormant within us, an inner vision [symphony] seeking completion in outer reality.[40]

As a child, I was enchanted with the notion that I could hear the universe in the whisperings of a shell.

Consciousness, personal unconsciousness (dreams), and collective unconsciousness (the gathered experience of universal history as it bears on *me right now*)—writing is strongest when it intimates all three.

Compose a passage whose surface reverberates thricely. Something is happening in the outer world while something more complex takes place in one's heart/mind/soul. This motion sways in a collective unconscious tide.

You don't have to spell everything out. You don't have to be right. Trust the reader's imaginative ear. If you are hearing well (and accurately recording what you hear) your reader will call forth what your words arouse in her and fill in the blanks.

DOODLE WITH YOUR EAR

. . . I think it's impossible not to get some sort of form if you don't think about it. If you do think about it, you can get chaos. But if you don't think about it, you get form. . . .[41]

When Wallace Stevens poetically rather than scientifically described an equestrian monument, his purpose was "without imposing, without reasoning at all, to find the eccentric at the base of design."[42]

Stevens used analogies and "imaginative identification" to arrive at his truth. Painters doodle. As Fairfield Porter reported:

When I was in high school, doing algebra or something, I would see the doodle [I'd made] and like the way it looked. It had a certain spontaneity and fresh-

ness; it had a certain shape. And I would think, I'll do it again, I'll copy that because I like it. I would copy it. But the copy wouldn't have that freshness. It was only chaotic.[43]

Try it. Doodle with your "ear." If you must, trick yourself into authenticity!

LISTENING TO THE WORLD

There is no need for you to leave the house. Stay at your table and listen. Don't even listen, just wait. Don't even wait, be completely alone and quiet. The world will offer itself to you to be unmasked; it can't do otherwise; in raptures it will writhe before you.

—*Franz Kafka*[44]

REALITY AS A SOURCE
OF REFLECTION

I was born on this plateau, this piece of ancient rock cra-
dled north and south by two seas. Its contours are im-
printed upon my inner eye [*ear*] in a way that time
cannot erase. And each time the windswept spaces of
the *Kavir* fill my vision, each time I see naked mountains,
whether in Arizona or Tehran, I feel it, I feel that sense of
completion.

—*Gelareh Asayesh*[45]

Our initial experience of (let's say) hearing is the first step
toward capturing and absorbing what we've heard. But
true hearing happens over time. Philosopher Maurice
Merleau-Ponty boiled the entire effort of modern painting
down to severing the adherence to the envelope of things.

Complete fidelity to an experience is impossible.
Bridging the gap between one's perception and one's rep-
resentation is seemingly beyond our grasp.

The imagining ear features this reality. Hovering

around the event, objective truth has an opportunity to mingle with the truth of one's own "sensations."

Kew Gardens, for example, is a snail's-eye view of the passersby of its flower bed. Imagine the bits and pieces of snatched conversation that passed through Virginia Woolf's brain as she entered a mollusk's universe and restricted her hearing to its. Fragmented, scrambled time and space, fractured, random thought and speech—her choices eventually based, mollusk or no, on "mind time that simulates the way beings experience the linear flow of sequence and consequence."[46]

The element of otherness inherent in the spontaneity of the present moment speaks to the dynamism (or tension) between the ear and soul of a writer.

Ceaseless motion is established. Distancing itself from static reality—because reality isn't like that—the imagining ear's volleying rhythms add a dimension of things-as-they-are.

"I HAVE TO LEARN TO
THINK ABOUT BOUDIN AS
IF I WERE A COW!"

Life is not fixed. Hearing life authentically is bound to be amazing, unpredictable, jazzy.

What a writer hears constantly shifts along with how she hears it. (Think of an amoebae endlessly squirming around.) As soon as something congeals, the imagining ear wilts. When healthy, its tensions—rigor and improvisation, observation and expression, chaos and order, science and poetry—ebb and flow in ever-unexpected partnerships.

A complex, provocative heterodoxy, heightened by the imagining ear's scanning, is chewed up, spit out, and left to be dealt with. Somehow.

Preparing for a show, Pissarro said, "I have to go into retreat within myself like the monks of the past, and quietly, patiently elaborate the *oeuvre*."[47]

THE YOGA OF
POSITIVE LISTENING

"The problem with listening, of course, is that we don't. There's too much noise going on in our heads, so we never hear anything. . . . In the same way, we don't see, and in the same way we don't feel, we don't touch, we don't taste," says composer/performer Philip Glass.[48]

Being a composer is about listening. Being a writer (young Robert Frost discovered while still a farmer) is about the "imagining ear." "Deep listening" (which is not just an auditory sensation but a matter of the whole person) is the way a writer positions herself in the world.

A word *is* God, not merely a signifier. When we imagine a word, a part of us remembers precisely who we are. Being sacred, words hold tremendous and mysterious power. They need to be handled with mindfulness and respect.

Everything important is invisible. An object may exist and to the eye may be beautiful, but its gravity takes experience to appreciate.

Everything important is inaudible. The voice of our most powerful yearnings can only be heard by our inner, beingness-is-one ear.

Discordant tempos, contrasts between geometrized (architectural) sound units versus the effervescence of natural ones, softly perceived by the imagining ear, rendered softly by the writer's hand, reveal that even within the infinity of the divine, one cannot escape the contingency of the mundane. Which contingency (how it shapes itself) is particular to each writer, though its mark (her "acoustic birthmark") may be invisible.

"PRIMROSE BURN THEIR YELLOW FIRES WHERE GRASS AND ROADWAY MEET"

Are we to gaze at the moon and flowers with the eye alone? To lie awake anxiously through the rainy night, and stand before the petal-strewn, drenched shadow of the trees, yearning after what has passed, this indeed . . .

—*Priest Kenko*[49]

Poets speak of an "attitude of listening," of "clarifying the mind's ear" so that one hears not only what is present but what is evoked by what is present—mountain depths in a cuckoo's cry, falling leaves in the flurry of night rain, a lake's glassy surface in a swarming mass of mosquitoes.[50] Listening suggests sound, but we listen just as intently to temperature, taste, texture. The panorama of a hidden peak, the tensioned-saffron in the robe of our Abbot's root-guru, the silky surface of a glacier whose slush covers our boots, the pedigreed great-grandfather of a newly born foal, a thousand cranes, an African-drum skin, orchid feathers, fresh spring water—each has its overtone, pitch, harmony, whose unique inflection is apprehended by our mental ear's imagination.

Poets, writers, even loved ones will leave what's most important out—not out of carelessness, but out of respect. "Here are the bare essentials," they ostensibly say. "Create from them *your* history, *your* past, *your* heart's desire."

PAINTING COLD,
PAINTING SPRING

Painting cold, Pissarro plays with the subtle interaction of atmosphere, light, energy, and the pacing of movement within a crisp, autumn morning. Everything seems to be arrested. Immobilizing cold is balanced by the sun gently warming the landscape. Purple shadows through tall, bare, scraggly tree trunks— alongside tendrils of smoke, horses, people, and tiny threads of unpainted canvas—add volume to both the objects and the paint.[51]

Painting spring, Pissarro paints a landscape in spring. No metaphors. No symbols. The bending sower simply attends the earth. His gestures are self-referential, self-sufficient, non-sentimental, and stand for nothing outside himself in the present moment.

How does a painter paint cold? How does a painter paint spring? How does a writer hear cold, spring, rocks, carrots, ragamuffins, so thoroughly that they become a "given?"

They feel. Using their imagining ear (in Pissarro's words their *own* "sensation"), they "inhale" an energetic field and "exhale" a formed thing.

We get no letter from the world of emptiness, but when you see the plant flower, when you hear the sound of bamboo hit by the small stone, that is a letter from the world of emptiness.[52]

ABSOLUTE LIBERTY

He let many things pass without being duped.

— I Ching

In expressing satisfaction to his son at having completed *Seated Peasant, Sunset,* Pissarro defines his Wordsworthian-like method: to recollect truth via the tranquility of memory.

Memory, he felt, is more accurate than direct observation. Just as his figures tend to be absent-minded, Pissarro himself grows vague. Musing, dreaming, contemplating, he distances himself from his first "take." "Really Impressionism," he says, is "nothing but a pure theory of observation, without losing hold of fantasy, liberty, or grandeur. . . ."[53]

His figures convey no message. They are absorbed in their reverie or chore. What's important is their unfathomability. His dreamers and their dreams equal "ABSOLUTE LIBERTY."

"ABSOLUTE LIBERTY" equals one's own "sensation"—abiding in this, despite any other concern. The tool is the Master; the imagining ear is a writer's tool (her *own* "sensation").

What gives grace to a picture? It is an unconscious re-flection of the grace in the artist's mind.[54]

In his last paintings, Harlen Hubbard's work takes on the I-Thou quality of a conversation. The subject *speaks* to the artist; the artist *speaks back* by way of his painting. "Good painting is done in a kind of trance," Hubbard says. The painter (writer) stands aside and an outside power takes over.

By eavesdropping on the landscapes of paradise (or "heaven" as he sometimes puts it), Hubbard sees the timelessness in time and the things of time, and hears the pulse of their silence.

"When I paint a landscape, I try to paint heaven, and my joy at being there," he stresses. Hubbard's paintings are not scenes. The world is not scenery, but earthly places that one absorbs and then molds with one's hands.

He had measured the distances of the river with oars hundreds of times. As herdsman and forager, he had climbed the hills and walked the ridges hundreds of times. The country was present to him in its abounding and intricate detail. He knew it not just as "scenes," but as substance and in all his nerves.[55]

Painting for Hubbard was an indispensable way to realize and connect with his dwelling place. Far from treating a subject (the stance in itself to him was disrespectful), Hubbard allowed painting to carry him ever more deeply into the presence of his homeland.

Who we are is not contained within our skin, but extends, via the senses (hearing) into our surroundings. "Home" is really the "country of the mind"—the land identified to memory by deeply felt associations. Whether a portion of land (*to you*) is mere scenery or home depends on this invisible landscape.

. . . the world is not sitting for its portrait, but is turned away, as if thinking of something else. This is a quality of any quiet rural landscape, noticeable to anybody who looks long and quietly enough. . . . The artist is almost breathlessly aware that he must not paint—

he must not think—in any way that would disturb the integrity of what is before him: the farm buildings and small fields and their human inhabitants occupying what seem to be their natural places, the artifacts all modestly scaled, all having a certain beauty and dignity that denote their belonging where they are, and over it all the brooding quietness of the timelessness that contains time.[56]

Rather than paint the landscape, Hubbard *hears* the landscape dictate its own portraiture.

A CÉZANNE
IS A MOMENT

Express no message, represent no canon, abandon all literary ambition. Be neither idealistic, materialistic, socialistic, nor scholastic. Spurn any program. Simply hobble along in your *own* "sensation."

Is that what it takes for a writer to stay sincere?

Duret, in a letter to Pissarro encouraging him to pursue nature (landscapes with animals) as his primary subject, said, ". . . a beautiful picture by you is something with an absolute presence."[57] Pissarro, meanwhile, buttering hay into thick voluminous sheaves, was deftly painting clouds—scumbling dry, frothy whirling masses—leaving huge gaps of unprimed, unbrushed, light brown canvas.

Sincerity has no formula, which is to say that everything emerges from a "shimmering matrix of changing conditions." "Whoever sees contingency," declared Gautama, "sees dharma; and whoever sees dharma sees Buddha."

Your imagining ear with its radar mind, scanning the

universe for up-to-the-minute fluctuations, is your own private news anchor reporting live from eruption's epicenter. Even silence is vibrant. A snow scene in the dead of cold bristles with noise.

Just as frugality is not cheapness but appraising one's needs and meeting them without a lot of excess, simplicity is not sentimentality. The simple answer to a problem is direct, unadorned, and truthful.

Regarding art, sentimentality is the most corrupt [Pissarro felt]. He was wary of his figures saying too much, horrified at "orange-blossom art which makes delicate women swoon."[58] Because it is contrived, out to create an effect, therefore manipulative (and, at its core, aggressive), making "delicate women" or anybody else "do" anything is contrary both to frugality and simplicity (which, by definition, are self- and situational-referential).

Some genres are more susceptible to sentimentality than others. If you paint (write) a portrait, it is difficult to ignore the expression (sentiment) of your subject (though not impossible).

Cities can relate an entire philosophy; a columnar kiosk can be a synecdoche for now.

SHADOW AND STRUCTURE

To observe without evaluating is the highest form of intelligence.

—J. Krishnamurti

A commonly held belief about Impressionism is that its intention was to paint light. More precisely, Impressionists painted light insofar as it produced its inevitable counter effect: shadow. Shadows define and distribute light just as light projects and constructs shadows (the silvery patches of sun pricking the ground through a row of pines). These constant fluctuations are perceptible within an unchanging contextual reality (rivers, trees, farmland, houses).

What the Impressionists did with light, writers do with sound. Through sound, they derive non-sound and vice versa. These perpetually changing, yet acoustically unavoidable marks of things, become apparent in a context of tranquility.

Tranquility is impervious to street noise. Its enemies

are aggression, judgment, criticism, bigotry, aggrandize-
ment, egotism, self-centeredness. "Ahhhh let's . . ." is its
anthem. "You better . . ." its death knoll. Facing a firing
squad, one only hears a bullet.

"THE MONGOLS, I LIKED
TO THINK, HAD RETREATED
TO THE OUTBACK WITH
THEIR ESSENTIAL NOMADIC
WILDNESS INTACT"

———

When Cézanne's first show was ill-received, Pissarro was upset. Upholding their kinship, he insightfully wrote that though they were always together, each independently upheld his own "sensation."

"Sensation" is the crucial word. The idea corresponds to the physical (instinctual) experience plus the idiosyncratic and singular feeling of explicit relation to oneself. It names the place where artists (writers) hold a vital intelligence, most easily accessed when the body is in motion.

In repetitive motion, one both thinks and feels. Spiritual, emotional, and psychological information (bound up in one's body) can be expressed and released.

I learned to see dance, by knowing it in my body.[59]

Carving into words the volleying rhythms pulsing through the body's silent continuum is the essence of a writer's craft.

———

"Art is not reality," Flaubert once said. It is a selective process. In a series, for example, each component is called for by an inner necessity (heard by the artist), whose artistic task is to "summarize humanity."

"Neither wallflowers nor roses are interesting in themselves." The only interesting thing is the artist's manner of rendering them.

Steadfastness, willpower, and one's *own* "sensations" (stripped of "alien concerns") filter reality before it becomes art.

What are "alien concerns"? Buying into an "aristocracy of subject matter," politicizing one's work, seeing [hearing] inauthentically or in a contrived way, fearing (or even being concerned) for judgment, valuing result over process to name a few. One's *own* "sensations" (having them, knowing one has them, and being able to articulate them artistically)—this skill comes after a long, painful struggle. It is not simply disheveled indulgence in wild excitement; Pissarro said, "It is the freedom to impose on oneself one's own law, one's own regulations or limitations, one's own pictorial reflection, and one's own process of selection. This is, strictly speaking, the definition of autonomy (giving oneself one's own law)—a concept absolutely central to anarchy."[60]

Artists are always anarchists.

WORDS SAY US

———

I went and leaned my forehead against the ancient stones [the Kotel, the Western Wall of the Great Temple in Jerusalem] and felt waves of energy coming out of the Wall. Men in black garb were rolling out Torahs on tables from the caves at the north end. Prayer groups were gathering around every table with its Torah, and I heard the sounds of each prayer service starting up one after the other. They came together in a fugue, funneling all the prayers out of the stones and up to Heaven.[61]

In its earliest context, prayer occurred at the nexus of the self and communal consciousness. Jazz musicians who improvise on a standard understand. A mime or a poet writing a sonnet positions herself similarly. It's a way of hearing yourself along with everyone else.

Listen with your imagining ear. It may be to the evening song of a coyote, the lament of a mangled doll, the blessing and encouragement of the gods in your Tibetan *thangka*, the advice or warning of your power animal. Your dog may confess that it's going to die soon, your father that his liver transplant has seen its best years. They talk. You *listen*, and transcribe. Later you can figure out the full implications of what you have heard.

Include the dimension of time—past, present, and future—and identify the constraints as well as freedoms that it imposes. Take charge of the tense you pick so that your emotion is matched to the ultimate effect you intend to create by your reverie.

GOD'S EARS

———

Like those of families, the fortunes of gods rise and fall. Hearing our devotion, their power builds. But the shadow can drop on the human side as well. When their mountains are violated, the gods flee, and all human endeavors go badly.

Mountains are gods' abode. When we visit, we ought to be polite. Since gods do not bestow benefits so much as listen to requests for them, a perspicacious seeker will speak softly, behave respectfully, protect the space from harm, portray a consciousness of humility. As hosts, gods are cognizant of their guests' safety and well-being. They derive enjoyment from providing benevolent protection.

Among Tibetan lamas, there is a hearing hierarchy (differing levels of ability to hear mystical forces) based on differing levels of self-discipline.

Writers too are pedigreed human beings. Our ears are

sharp, finely honed, and exquisitely sensitive. By applying small gestures of self-discipline, we pick up sounds other people miss.

"I CALL THEM BELCHER-SQUELCHERS. THEY GO *SLUG-TOOT, SLUG-TOOT, SLUG-TOOT.*"

[exercise]

An entire ecosystem can exist in the plumage of a bird.

—E. O. Wilson

There remains, in the old Keniston house, a scrapbook with pictures of the place and the work—including a photo of a trapped Northern Harrier caught eating a Heath Hen, the shocked hawk looking back over one wing while the Heath Hen is nothing more than a white sprawl of over-exposed light, a terrorized glare without substance.

[Describe this morning . . . something that you noticed, thought, or did since you got up.]

Neither "tooting" nor "old muldoon" captures the hypnotic moaning quality of several birds booming and droning at once. The o-o-o of the Heath Hen and the Greater Prairie-Chicken has been compared to the sound of blowing air over the lip of an empty glass bottle as well as to the notes of faraway tugboats. One writer said of droning Heath Hens, "It sounded as if a lot of lonesome little night winds had taken to crying whoo-oo-o in ragtime, mingled with whistles of syncopated measure. . . ." [62]

[Rework your passage changing the emphasis. For example, use the same elements but switch the focus and possibly make a different point.]

Brightly yellow-eyed and jittery, the Ivory-bill appeared vividly strange, nearly Mesozoic, as it pounded and drilled the rotting trees of shadow-wet forests and jerked its long, white-billed head this way and that, as if it were the alert guardian of the sloughs. The Ivory-bill conveyed a manic glory as it hopped up and down the sides of cypresses and hackberries or launched off into flight. Upon seeing an Ivory-bill for the first time, one naturalist wrote that he felt "tremendously impressed by the majestic and wild personality of this bird, its vigor, its almost frantic aliveness." This, the King of the Woodpeckers.

The plumage seemed elemental: black bodies with white stripes stretching from the side of the head along the neck and down the back; when the bird perched, a patch of white on the wings' trailing edge showed like a knight's bright culet; the female's recurved crest displayed only jet-black, while the male sported a crest of blood red that gleamed in sunlight shafting through the forest canopy.[63]

[Read your above passages aloud listening for something that you hadn't previously been aware of. Write about *that*—hearing it, your feelings about hearing it, its implications, repercussions, reverberations.]

In the day's first ample light, we in the blind could see the birds' soft brown bodies, the fences, a stock tank, and a pair of frozen ponds. We heard the pitch change—a bit higher, I thought—oiue. And wohoo— *perhaps a female (or hen) skulked nearby, but we*

couldn't see whether one elicited this peculiar outcry.
The males (or cocks) purred with laughter. I could see
one chunky shape then another and another. Rapid
cackles—"petulant" said one naturalist—like a chit-
ter, then a whoop. *John confirmed what I had sus-*
pected—that males "whoop" only when they think
females are present. (Sometimes males "act" like fe-
males, causing mistaken whoops—*a rather apt word,*
in such a case.) And the cackles are more like male con-
versations, John explained. Guy talk.[64]

[Return to your subject, experiencing it with your inner ear. Become the vessel of what emerges. Translate that
into words.]

Over and over, for many exhilarating, exhausting
minutes, the males erected their pinnae in very spiffy
black V's—lusty little devil horns—then bowed for-
ward so their bellies parallel the earth. They spread
their tails, pointed their wings to the ground, bobbed
their necks with a quick jerk and inflated their orange
air sacs, swelling like party favors. The birds charged
and squatted hard down, again. They jumped, again,
turning full circles or half circles in the air; then landed,
nonplussed or affronted. Some males turned partial

circles while stamping their feet on the ground, nature's most perfect tantrum or celebration or both. It seemed that no vanity of posture, no absurdity of motion, could finally uncoil this profuse, enraged desire.[65]

LISTENING TO WORDS

For isn't it not that we "find our voice" as poetry teachers are so fond of saying, but rather that voices find us, and perhaps we welcome them? Is not poetry a dance from possession to possession—"obsession" in the full sense the word had in nineteenth-century magick? We are "ridden" as by the gods.

—Diane di Prima[66]

Yah of *Yahweh* means "God." It also means "word." A daughter of God is also a daughter of the word. Could hearing a word be related to hearing God or hearing the God in one's self?

A word is. It also signifies something. The form of signification makes its own separate statement. Three sequential words have thus acted thricely. Yet we listen (ordinarily) to a fourth, more linear dimension. ("*What* did you say?")

While we are busy construing this fourth dimension, the other three have their way with us. The word's "*yah* aspect" will not be confined to the material realm. The power of a word inherently supersedes the power of humans to measure it. By osmosis, it infiltrates our body/mind/soul.

The "something else" also has a "*yah* aspect." While God, for example, is a powerful word, what it signifies may be even more powerful because of its cumulative mystical, cultural, historical, psychological memory. Dreams, reveries, fantasies waft through this fleeting cloud bed.

William James objected to describing the continuously changing stream of human thought with railway-like nouns ("train" or "chain"). Virginia Woolf agreed. People, she insisted, "don't and never did feel or think or dream for a second in that way; but all over the place."[67]

A word's aura signifies a universe, access to which is contained in its aura. We step in gingerly, and the sound spins us to a vortex of an unknown galaxy of other meaningful sounds.

With practice, writers can learn to screen out the dictionary and relax into the muscularity of each word's unique routine. Pure listening keeps a word afloat. No cumbersome argument. Deep listening (with our imagining ear) keeps a word (and its compatriots) free.

Kutastha Chaitanya, the ever-pure reflection of Spirit, is incarnate in the birth of great souls, says the Hindu Yogi Paramahansa Yogananda. But everyone can learn to bring the "ever-pure reflection of Spirit" into consciousness. Once it is fully present, one can dedicate it to the benefit of all beings. Dedication (giving the fruits of one's actions away) both empties them and makes them entirely one's own.

Prayer is talking to God. But *you* have to *hear* your prayer before you can expect God to hear it. As it washes through your being, you *hear* God *hear*—viscerally. You *hear* yourself *hearing* God *hear.*

Prayer in Hebrew or Latin or Sanskrit—even if, as you chant, you are unfamiliar with these languages—is potent nonetheless.

> . . . *the closer we get to being present, the closer we get to God. Being present is God's name, all breath sounds, no consonant stops—"Yuh. Heh. Wuh. Heh"—all process*

and flow, no stopping points, absolute being, absolute becoming.[68]

The name of God is the only way to express present-tense being in the Hebrew language.

After Jacob wrestles all night with a "dark stranger," God tells him, "Your name will no longer be Jacob, but rather 'Yisrael,' because you have struggled with God and you have prevailed."

Facing a blank page, writers "wrestle with God" daily. "Who am I who struggles so boldly? Who invited me to fight? How can language be such a life-and-death battle?" Words and the things that precede them are deeply mysterious.

COLOR MUST
BE THOUGHT

All art worthy of the name is religious. Whether it is made of lines or of colors, if this creation is not religious, it is not art. It is nothing more than a document, an anecdote.

—*Matisse*[69]

Color must be thought, filtered through the imagination. Without imagination, beautiful colors are hard to construct.

Good color sings. Good lines (drawn or written) know precisely where they wish to enter or exit a portrait.

By superimposing love on the recollected moment, a writer adds the presence of God. (That's why words can be lastingly moving.) A writer listens with her imagining ear to God's presence in her heart.

That's her skill—to be affected more than others by "absent things," and to express them in words as they arise. A writer draws her heart close to that of another— lets herself slip—into the "beat" of another.

According to Jewish law, the unspoken name of God must never be haphazardly discarded. Synagogues have bins built right into their walls where old books and papers bearing God's name are stored. When enough accumulate, they are added to the casket of a rabbi or scholar and buried with dignity.

While words empower us through our use of them, we likewise transform and empower words. Not just etymologically. ". . . we change the words as well when we use them, the way the shoe of a small child begins to express the shape of that child's foot when it's well worn," said Rabbi Alan Lew.[70]

The great koan of prayer, the present-day paradox, is that this prayer service works so well, and the particular text of the prayer service—every word—derives a tremendous sanctity from all the Jewish souls who have said these words for several thousand years.[71]

Scriptures are sacred. The consciousness one brings to their study and recitation matters. It's not about belief. It's about energy, its transference and power to create transformation.

Each morning an orthodox Jew "lays tefillin":

You spell out one of God's names—Shaddai—with the straps of the tefillin on your hand, so when you put them on, you are literally binding yourself to the name of God . . . this prayer practice would change the texture of the rest of the day. I would visualize the words as an energy exchange—the words going up to God and God's attention coming down. Prayer began bringing me to the same place my Zen practice had taken me.[72]

A word, after all, is empty — therefore spacious.

Overemphasizing the meaning of a word strips it of its power. A word (its sound alone) can change a mind, a heart, a soul. Hearing one affects eternity.

OM MANI
PADME HUM

QUESTION: What *is* an "imagining ear"?
ANSWER: The Hopi idea of "finding the voice of the earth
and singing a note in harmony with it, resonating with the
earth, and becoming, thereby, an adjunct to the earth."[73]

Tibetan is a language without subjects. While English
clearly distinguishes between objects and actions (nouns
and verbs), many Tibetan words are both. One who
thinks in Tibetan, therefore, has little difficulty understanding that things are events. She *hears* their process.

So Om mani padme hum *is the safeguarding vision of
the compassion of Avalokiteshvara extending around
us. It's like the All-state commercial, but with Avalokiteshvara's thousands of hands holding us up in moments of death and rebirth.*[74]

Om mani padme hum. Om mani padme hum. Om mani padme hum. Om mani padme hum. Tibetans whirl the mantra—wisdom, compassion, love, bliss around their minds using prayer wheels to expand the field of energy.

Our writing minds should always be in a positive flow, in an inner *murmuring* like water.

Hearing your voice with your "imagining ear" *is* hearing *Om mani padme hum. Om mani padme hum* is the Sanskrit translation of *your* essential nature. *Om mani padme hum* is a code for the part of you that already knows God, that recognizes instantly the sound of one hand clapping. You *hear* yourself doing it all the time.

TEAR IT DOWN

Inner silence. The sound of Om. There's no difference. The latter ripples through the universe in one continuous flow. The former ripples through our heart of hearts.

Grasshoppers and crickets use their *ears* (on the grasshopper's abdomen, the cricket's front knees) to *listen* for potential mates, rivals, predators. All are detected via a thin membrane on a sensitive receptor. Our language can be select like the life/death communications of crickets and grasshoppers, if we aim our words at the heart of the other.

Body, mind, and soul are partially furnished with words. Using language carelessly is disruptive to one's sense of cleanliness, order, beauty, comfort. Repercussions of carelessness taint our lives and those of untold others.

So it is with words tossed about instead of selected according to design and offered in a dedicated spirit of service.

If we create a trace in someone's mind because of what we say or do, that trace may last for a lifetime.[76]

Determination is required to put practice into action. First we sense we "know"—an inner correspondence to the "suchness" we hear in every bird's chirp. The chirps dissolve in our mind's ear. The "knowing" gets deeper, filters into our blood. Failure to abide in what is now our "Way," is what Aitken-roshi calls "disloyal."

"POETS ARE NEVER MAD—EVERYBODY ELSE IS"[77]

Monks have always recognized reading as a bodily experience, primarily oral. The ancients spoke of masticating the words of scripture in order to fully digest them. Monastic "church" reflects a whole-body religion, still in touch with its orality, its music. In the midst of today's revolution in "instant communication" I find it a blessing that monks still respect the slow way that words work on the human psyche.[78]

When the Benedictine-inspired poet Kathleen Norris worried to her oblate director about her response (inspired writing) to *lectio divina* (literally "holy reading"), he said, "What do you mean? You're *doing it!*" He called her writing "active *lectio.*" *Lectio* and writing are similar, he said, because both are grounded in the body.

Being with monks, listening to them read their scriptures, is like "imbibing language . . . at full strength,"

Norris comments. Why is listening in a monastic setting different from listening in ordinary life?

Trappists and Benedictines practice silence. Within a context of silence, a sound (a word) means something. A person hearing one will likely pay attention.

In ordinary life, sounds and words are cheap. Paying attention almost makes one a pariah. To steal silence (let's say for a task that requires concentration), one develops outlaw strategies (hiding, white-lying, disappearing).

Monks and poets (America's archetypal outcasts) recognize the transformative power lurking in simple things (like words). "Let words work the earth of my heart," they pray. Perhaps culture as a whole no longer feels safe with such potentially dangerous toys.

THE DAILY LIFE OF
PROPER LANGUAGE

You should clearly understand that because everyday language is the whole universe, the whole universe is everyday language.

—*Zen Master Dogen*[79]

Liturgy makes the invisible visible (the unhearable hearable). The Zen liturgy is a good example because in it nothing is explained. (It proceeds as if everyone knows.) To hear, we must shift away from ordinary listening, abandon our usual (dualistic) reference point.

Intimacy is the secret. (All liturgy is secret.) Secrets remain "dark to the mind but radiant to the heart."[80]

Everyday life, everyday language, everyday listening become liturgy when we take full responsibility for them, for example, when through intimacy with our actions, our actions become clarified and concrete.

In the end, a writer's entire life (including her writing) is liturgy.

THE "THOUGHT OF HEARING"
KILLS HEARING.
THE ONLY HEARING THERE IS
HAS NEVER NOT EXISTED.

Restraint played a role in the particular kind of intimacy that Robert Frost developed in his personal relationship with language. "You've got to feel it, the emotion," he said, "but you hold back from saying it, keep it in. The power is there."[81]

One must hear stillness, not agitation. Again and again, Frost removed himself from outside obligations so that he could "face the blank page . . . listen to the inner voice that was caught, at times accidentally, as he walked in the woods or sat, idly, expecting nothing."[82]

Mixed in the "caught" was over-sound, an echo of intelligence that inevitably contributes to the universal bank of emotional and verbal music. For Frost, over-sound was tinged with resistance, with the human need to counter the downward drift toward darkness, the natural disintegration of the organic universe.

Robert Frost encouraged his students to use their *ears* in gathering material for compositions.

When you listen to a speaker, you hear words, to be sure—but you also hear tones. The problem is to note them, to imagine them again, and to get them down in writing.[83]

Frost elaborated:

When I began to teach, and long after I began to write, I didn't know what the matter was with me and my writing and with other people's writing. I recall distinctly the joy with which I had the first satisfaction of getting an expression adequate for my thought. I was so delighted that I had to cry. It was the second stanza of the little poem on the butterfly, written in my eighteenth year.

He discovered the sound in the mouths of people, "not merely [in] words or phrases, but [in] sentences—living things flying round, the vital parts of speech."[84]

Frost said that sentence-sounds are very precise, gathered by the ear from the vernacular. Writers don't invent them; rather, they catch them fresh from talk "where they grow spontaneously."

The best way to hear the vocal idiom or "posture" that connects every speaker to his language (a community of shared signals) is from voices behind a closed door (where you can't actually make out the words).

What separates and connects the poet to this community is parsing. Two factors are always at work: the abstract possibility of the line and the poet's individual way of "breaking" the words across it.

Thus Frost never "recites" his poems. He "says" them. Sometimes, especially if they are new or short, he "says" them twice. "Would you like to *hear* me say that one again?"[85]

A word—its nativity, parentage, schooling (shaping/coming into its own), romance, marriage, offspring, indeed its entire astrology—is heard and participated in by Joyce.

Each word has a natal chart, twelve houses, ascendant (rising sign), and moon. Its planets may be squared. Its stars may be crossed. Times of oblivion, obfuscation, and fortune—the heritage of every member of the English lexicon—Joyce roots in the miasma of the ephemeris.

Sentient beings (for example, words) are born with a life plan—characteristic patterns and etymological proclivities—that become its destiny to fulfill. Karmically, this is a path, a monogrammed map to freedom (full power). As one sets forth from bardo to a chosen incarnation, a rhythm is established. Joyce hears every syllable's cacophony and flow.

A few light taps upon the pane made him turn to the window. It had begun to snow again. He watched sleepily the flakes, silver and dark, falling obliquely against the lamplight. The time had come for him to set out on his journey westward. Yes, the newspapers were right: snow was general all over Ireland. It was falling on every part of the dark central plain, on the treeless hills, falling softly upon the Bog of Allen and, farther westward, softly falling into the dark mutinous Shannon waves. It was falling, too, upon every part of the lonely churchyard on the hill where Michael Furey lay buried. It lay thickly drifted on the crooked crosses and headstones, on the spears of the little gate, on the barren thorns. His soul swooned slowly as he heard the snow falling faintly through the universe and faintly falling, like the descent of their last end, upon all the living and the dead.[86]

We all have receptors and receptors have temperaments. Each attunes to certain situations and modes of behavior more readily than others. Joyce *hears* God's band.

"THE AMERICANS WERE ABLE TO PUT A MAN ON THE MOON BECAUSE THEY KNEW ENGLISH. THE SINHALESE AND TAMILS WHOSE KNOWLEDGE OF ENGLISH WAS POOR, THOUGHT THAT THE EARTH WAS FLAT."[87]

The mind is like a donkey. Control it though we will, it will bolt at the least expected (desirable) opportunity.

Human beings *will* reinvent "reality" according to what they can or cannot tolerate. "Facts" often are not "facts" but tips of icebergs that are censored, edited, poeticized.

Human lives *are* elliptical.

Michael Ondaatje wrote:

Drought since December.

All across the city men roll carts with ice clothed in sawdust. Later on, during a fever, the drought still continuing, his nightmare is that thorn trees in the garden send their hard roots underground towards the house climbing through windows so they can drink sweat off his body, steal the last of the saliva off his tongue.

He snaps on the electricity just before daybreak. For twenty-five years he has not lived in this country, though up to the age of eleven he slept in rooms like this—with no curtains, just delicate bars across the windows so no one could break in. And the floors of red cement polished smooth, cool against bare feet.

Dawn through a garden. Clarity to leaves, fruit, the dark yellow of the King Coconut. This delicate light is allowed only a brief moment of the day. In ten minutes the garden will lie in a blaze of heat, frantic with noise and butterflies.

Half a page—and the morning is already ancient.[88]

"*Listen,*" he so much as says. "I'm touching my life into words." First he *hears*. Then he masticates, metabolizes, evacuates the baser metal, placing a Houdini-like piece of gold on our pleasure platter.

A magician (of words), he pulls twenty-five (their equivalent power) out of a mere . . . one.

Ondaatje's ecstasy is infectious. Dragged by the undertow, we are pulled right in to the drone of his memories— plump, steady, bellow-like.

ONE FALLING LEAF IS
NOT JUST ONE LEAF;
IT MEANS
THE WHOLE AUTUMN

Ambiguity—calculated, deliberate, forthright—is the closest we ever get to reality, reasoned Virginia Woolf, for whom "poetic aspect" meant the whole possible stretch of meaning a word or phrase might generate. A writer's task, she wrote, is "to take one thing and let it stand for twenty."[89] Its degree of semantic density, its range of semantic resonance —writers are engineers of such calculations.

What are our tools? And what precisely are we measuring?

We know that while words lie, the truth isn't entirely ours until it is articulated. We know that the nature of intersubjectivity is ephemeral. We know that this demands a deeper connection with our listening. We listen, then listen to our listening, its emotionality, cadence, tightness. Then, like Virginia Woolf, we listen for the reality behind the appearance.

A writer is like God, entering the presence of her subject—not her actual life, but what living it must feel like.

Calculus (for a writer)? The imagining ear + silence + a word (or group of words) = the derivative of the evocation of the ineffable.

YIN LISTENING,
YANG LISTENING

On my leaves of words,
may the wind draw forth
a cold hue

—*Priest Shinkei*[90]

"Cold" (*yin*) refers to a poetry "ineluctably grounded on an apprehension of impermanence."[91] Shorn of all ornament, all desire to impress or seduce, "cold" ultimately describes poetry that is pure expression, beyond the dichotomy of subject and object.

"Warm" (*yang*) rhetoric, on the other hand, is where words, used inauthentically, interpose themselves between the mind and its object.

For Priest Shinkei, the undecorated and austere carve a path toward the original ground of being. Reducing language to a bare minimum allows it to stand as a transparent medium for one's quality of mind. A *yang listener*, therefore, would be one who interposes himself, his ideas, opinions, preconceptions, and judgments on what he hears. He may provide scintillating conversation, but even his cleverness is a screen through which others' words must impolitely force themselves.

A *yin listener* is empty. His ears are a vessel through which is poured the pure, undistilled, unadulterated voice of sentience. As he dedicates his body to the pristine transmission of the other's message, he himself is transformed.

"READ IT AGAIN, MOMMY!"

[exercise]

———

"Read it again, mommy! I want to hear it again, p-l-e-a-s-e," begs four-year-old sweetness, the soothing sound of the familiar arousing her imagining ear. Children love a story repeated. Their minds wallow in this pleasure.

Gertrude Stein uses repetition to *refresh* a word. One so used up it can no longer depict, she repeats and repeats till—dehydrated flower-like—it bursts into blossom. Joyce refurbished the word "yes" by similar tactics.

Language *is* the self, reflected and clothed in nouns and verbs and adjectives. But clothing gets worn, mirrors scar and shatter. First, find a word that has perished (an "endangered species" word) and resuscitate it. As you hear the life back into a word, record the ember-like flicker of memory that it rekindled.

UGLY *IS* BEAUTIFUL

In speaking of the Ilfracombe "lanes," she [George Eliot] says one should know the names of all the flowers clustered on their banks. "The desire [to know the names of all things] is part of the tendency that is now constantly growing in me to escape from all vagueness and inaccuracy into the daylight of distinct, vivid ideas." Eliot knows that merely to name an object "tends to give definiteness to our conception of it—we have then a sign that at once calls up in our minds the distinctive qualities which mark out for us that partic-ular object from all others."[92]

Without hate, love is not pure. Writing that favors, lies.

Practice honesty. Write a paragraph that lies in order to tell the truth more truthfully.

". . . AS THE SAP IN THE TWIGS"

[*e x e r c i s e*]

———

Just write very straight. Write so even a baby can understand.[93]

The *Tao* of language surges onward. Lie back. *Listen.* Allow yourself to drift.

Massage yourself with words. Improvise linguistically on what you *hear* your being report. Sway with the language that arises, on its own, unexpectedly, whispering (to your inner ear), "Write *me.* Write *me.* Pick *me* for your next sentence."

WORD "CANDY"

———

Sometimes we just like a word. The "tooth" of a word pleases our mouth. Toddlers teethe words—endlessly.

Pale chrome yellow, Milori green. Turkey red, cadmium . . .

Names vibrate. Beings vibrate. If they're in accord, the accord vibrates.

Think of a word as a hand composed of sound fingers. They pluck the body of a person whose ears vibrate with the essence of their sound.

EMPTY WORDS, REAL WORDS

———

Empty words have a task. Like a raft, they are freighted with intention, bringing us rapidly from here to there.

Real words stand for themselves. Their power lies in the unstated, unsaid, which the mind saturates with meaning.

Real words are queen bees. Empty words, drones. They slave away, then peter out.

An empty word carries baggage. A real word (radiant with light) flits through one's interior world, uplifting, magnetizing. When truth enters, certain behaviors become impossible. The silence of a real word guides one's conscience toward cosmic etiquette.

Use silence to weigh your words. Like wheat, the chaff will be borne windward. Silent minds are thin, spry, agile, pliable.

PROCESS

But there was more: the heart, the raw power inherent in art. Power generated out of discipline. Out of doing the same thing, day after day at the typewriter. In the studio. At the piano.

I remember in the 70s, hearing an interview with Pablo Casals on the radio. It had been done shortly before he died. The interviewer, a young reporter, none too bright, asked, "Mr. Casals, to what do you attribute your extraordinary success?" Or some such. And Pablo Casals answered in his careful, particular English: "Every day, since I was twelve, I play all my major and minor scales." The young reporter evidently didn't find this too interesting, was going on in his brisk way to the next question, when Pablo Casals cut him short, interrupted him in the middle of a word: "Did you hear me young man?—Every day, since I was twelve, I play all my major and minor scales."

Something he earnestly wanted to get across before he died. To whoever could hear it.[94]

BASIC IRRELEVANCE

Are monks and hippies and poets relevant? No, we're deliberately irrelevant. We live with an ingrained irrelevance which is proper to every human being.

—*Thomas Merton*[95]

In Chinese, the word, *shin,* for heart and mind is the same. For Zen Master Dogen, the concepts of body and mind are the same. "To study the self" means to be intimate with the self. Since the self is a writer's tool, a writer can realize writing by studying (being intimate with) her heart, body, and mind.

While your writing space may feel like a sanctuary, think of it as a furnace within which you forge the strength and self-confidence to fire your life into words. To function well, you must prepare carefully (all tools clean, ready, reachable), stay present (be available to receive writing), bow (ultimately all bows are to yourself), and leave no tracks (put away tools, tie up loose ends, leave the space spotless). This practice allows your writing to disappear (become "ingrained irrelevance").

Your writing time must be regular, because you need to foster stability. Stability is a vow. It means there is no vow higher than the one that you've made to yourself to write and witness your writing.

"YOU CAN WHIP OUR CREAM BUT YOU CAN'T BEAT OUR MILK"

It was from him, and from Moses, his brother, from Nick Cikovsky and Taubes, from Joseph Floch and Hans Boehler, workers all with a socialist mentality toward art, that I learned that you did the work come rain or shine. Whether or not there was inspiration for it. You did it, and didn't judge it, and did some more. Industrious, painstaking, careful, the routine itself was the support. What you built on. What sustained you.[96]

Anything done with a spirit of dedication, day after day, tames the body. Daily practice (obedience) quiets habitual, chaotic thoughts with which we have identified, falsely. Until these heavy-energy voices are under our control, subtler voices, also within us but harder to access, cannot be heard above the ruckus.

> . . . *listening for the eruptions of grace into one's life—often from unlikely sources—is a "quality of attention" that both monastic living and the practice cultivate.*[97]

To listen for the eruptions of grace, we must attune to the wisdom held deep within our body and use it to actuate what we hear. Quality listening (and obeying) arouse openness and gratitude.

When an adult cannot remember her childhood, often it is because her parents were just "going through the motions" (listening to some "should" as opposed to listening to their child). Though a child may have her physical needs met, if her emotional and psychological need for attunement (the "touch" of God, the point of connection, the "sign" that God has *heard*) is not, nothing sticks. When she begins to wake up (glimpse her true nature), she looks back on a blank world.

—————

"Is there anything you can't do?" George Crane asked his teacher, Tsung Tsai, noticing Tsung Tsai accomplished anything he wanted. Tsung Tsai replied, "No. Everything is the same. Just concentration."

One dawn, at a temple in Mongolia, seven monks crossed the courtyard, beads in hand, for their morning service. Tsung Tsai, who had been sitting on a stone bench throughout the night, rose to follow. George wrote:

I didn't follow. I couldn't. That I didn't feel worthy angered me. I don't need this guilt, I thought. Or this devotion. I refuse. Then the sutras began, and the great sound of life washed over me.

"Doesn't matter," Tsung Tsai said when I told him why I had not joined him for morning practice. "Buddhism, the real Buddhism is practice. Any moment must be practice. Any moment must be true." [99]

Toward the end of the journey, Tsung Tsai was on the verge of death but getting up anyway for his morning practice:

GEORGE: "Maybe you should rest."

TSUNG TSAI: "You rest, Georgie. Sleep. Anything. I cannot. I am a monk. Practice is my life."

GEORGE: "I'm with you. I'll do everything you do."

TSUNG TSAI: "You cannot. You make wrong. Completely no good."

(meaning "You can't fake it. Practice and truth are the same.")

George reflected:

Get to know what you're doing so well you don't know what you're doing, was the mantra I had adopted. . . . But every time I tried sitting I couldn't stay quiet. Meditation made me nauseous. . . .

Then I would go home to my life as an indigent poet. I was writing a poem a day. It was my religion. All I cared about.[100]

The unresolved elements in one's life and in the life of our parents repeat themselves till we get them right. Like a reoccurring dream, they arise from a place of tension. Awareness (consciousness) is the way to loosen their grip.

Awareness, like a blessing, comes to us freely. A point of focus is useful because it soothes our listening mind. But anything can be a point of focus.

God lives where *we* are. *Our* sacred space is God's address. Reading, thinking, writing, being—done with intentional consciousness—brings us closer to God because it brings us closer to our self in the present moment.

An *oryoki* is a set of three nestled bowls, chopsticks, spoon, and cleaning utensil, all cozily wrapped in a cloth that serves as a placemat for Zen monks during silent *zendo* meals. The little stack is housed to the right of each monk's seat. When the meal bell sounds, within cushion-reach is everything one needs to pray, eat, and clean up afterward.

The meal ritual is flawless thanks, in part, to the impeccably designed *oryoki*, but the design comes not so much from food as from listening.

Its beauty, elegance, and explicitness teach us how to live.

Once in place, it takes no special effort. It is faceless in the flow of the event. But the event (like any other in a writer's life) is enhanced by razor-sharp tools.

"What are the imagining ear's tools?" Respect, knowledge of one's materials, and a willingness to abide in PROCESS.

How do we sharpen them? By deepening our intuitive understanding of the relationship between the parts of a thing. (This informs the choice an artist makes intrinsic to the need of her work to move in a certain direction.)

Balanchine, for example, likes to work on the finale first. "Then I know where I'm going, where's the end," he said. "You have to know where you're going. If you start on the road, and you don't know where you're going, you never arrive anywhere."[101]

Any idea, modified over time, becomes more complex. Without an engagement with PROCESS, how will one's judgment of what is necessary (of just enough or the right amount) be accurate?

Genuine expressions must be self-existing, born within "me."

Personality inflects not only the selection, but also the organization of the selection from a particular point of view. If you want to do more than that, you have either to arrange and organize your selection (juxtapose its parts) in a pattern nobody has ever imagined before or do something altogether new (that nobody has ever imagined before).

This involves a kind of remembering—the imagining ear's vague yet total kind of remembering. I don't use myself to realize the world. The world uses me to realize me, which is the same as using me to realize it.

"BEFORE THE BEGINNING OF A POEM"/"AFTER THE END OF A POEM"

If you are going deeply into poetry, give your whole self to it—go the whole hog. Too many take it carefully, and fail. If it is to be your life, make everything else subordinate to it.

—Robert Frost to Daniel Smythe,
December 21, 1940[102]

One of Frost's poems, "The Ingenuities of Debt," was written five decades earlier than it was published. Typically, it lingered in Frost's folder of unfinished poems. In this case, it lingered largely because its meaning turns on an invented inscription from a long-destroyed city in the Middle East, and Frost had trouble getting a good enough line to fit here. It took him forty years to find: "Take care to sell your horse before he dies/The art of life is passing losses on."

In a letter of encouragement to Louis Untermeyer

(who had recently purchased a farm), Frost referred to "the stray souls who from incohesiveness feel rarely the need of the forum for their thoughts of the market for their wares and produce."

> They raise a crop of rye, we'll say. To them it is green manure. They plow it under. They raise a crop of endives in their cellar. They eat it themselves. That is they turn it under. They have an idea. Instead of rushing into print with it, they turn it under to enrich the soil. Out of that idea they have another idea. Still they turn that under. What they finally venture doubtfully to publication with is an idea of an idea of an idea.[103]

In his poem "Build Soil," the essential point concerns plowing under the first crops, letting the land go fallow, not stripping the soil but enriching it. It makes good sense in both farming and writing. (Frost was perpetually drawn to the alliance between the two.)

"Plowing under" swivels the "pressure" away from outside forces and onto one's self, so that one becomes one's own "pressure cooker." It is difficult enough to hear one's incipient emergent rhythms, next to impossible to hear them with an orchestra around. For this reason, Frost hated goals.

No matter how deeply cherished, goals behave in our psyche like outside forces. Instead, Frost claimed, "All that makes a writer is the ability to write strongly and directly from some unaccountable and almost invincible personal prejudice."[104]

"... WHEN I LISTENED CAREFULLY I COULD HEAR THE OPEN FLESH OF THAT FRUIT SING"

I have come to know that good farming is not so much about the broad strokes and big ideas. It grows from the confluence of millions of details.

—*Michael Ableman*[105]

"My grandparents were farmers and they emphasized technique," said urban farmer Michael Ableman, who, while self-admittedly lacking training, schooling, credentials, and books, had his grandparents' inspiration.[106] Like them, he intended to become an agricultural master. Over time, he discovered, it was more important to learn how to see.

Seeing happens in layers—as do smelling, tasting, touching, hearing. Beneath the stirring reds of an apple, for example, are various shades of green or yellow. Judges of world-class orchids claim that fragrance notes (the base ones at the bottom) reveal themselves gradually through the top and middle levels.

Fragrances also have memories . . . and fingerprints. Each flower of an orchid sends out a fragrance message to attract a certain insect. Other insects don't understand.

There is a "secret inside things," wrote Frost.[107] A writer must cultivate it, just as she cultivates silence. To penetrate a pear, we must fix ourselves before it until its voice whispers in our inner ear its never-before-heard sweetness.

We ask a question, which is not answered. But something else happens. Our question becomes a statement or, even better, an exclamation. The question is a caveat: "Dare I be so bold as to present my heart's truth?"

—

The patriarchal cultures equate male and female with sun and moon, light and dark, and life and death, while the Tantrics and Tibetans take the opposite tack, woman with sun and man with moon.

—*Robert Thurman*[108]

As soon as we think we know something, it disappears—including ourselves. Before we reach the end of the sentence, we're no longer the person who started it.

A tentative stance is more apt to be correct.

Tentativeness has a wide girth. You can both know and not know, be engaged and aware, yet fully open to the unexpected. Tentativeness is receptive (vulnerable) as opposed to authoritative (certain). Consequently, even if you, as writer (as listener), are fairly sure you know, cultivate an explorative state of mind.

Tentativeness takes courage. Spurning credentials, expertise, laurels, it gravitates instead toward the calm, centered, willing for anything.

"I've always been motivated by uncertainty. Ever since my days of finding my way home through the maze of Greek streets, I've counted on the unknown as my greatest teacher," said world-class mountaineer David Breashears.[109]

Great masters have ceaselessly recommended jumping off a cliff.

THE IMAGINING EAR
HEARS SOUNDS' "SOUL"

Felt more kinship to this notion of the artist, the writing—still do—than any model propagated in the art world, over the past three hundred years, or so. That the work is a part of the life, and you have leave to stop it, become a hobo, a mother, disappear, get sick, strung out, and you have leave to go back to it, and maybe you'll be as good as you were before. Maybe you'll be even better. Because in one sense, one part of yourself, you never do stop. What you don't control is the spirit, the voices, coming through you.[110]

"The deepest level of the mind, according to Buddha, is constantly in contact with body sensations," S. N. Goenka, a Burmese Vipassana Meditation teacher, is careful to teach. "And you find this by experience."

Musicians, surgeons, athletes, and dancers cultivate the quality of external movement that supports one-pointed attention. While drumming, dissecting, biking, bending—all are immersed in their body's continuous flow. The opposite quality (scattered, restless) knocks down the shields erected by the imagining ear (for example, writer's block).

"Think with your ears" is the writer's version of S. N. Goenka's instruction. The deepest level of the mind (from where our words originate) is connected to the pen by the imagining ear.

Strength equals focus. Focus equals trust. Trust is not owned. It just drifts through the universe and, like surfers, we wait, tread for a bit, catch a wave, ride to shore buoyantly. Waiting we know. We hear our knowing into existence long before it wells up from the ocean's depths.

"THE REQUIREMENTS OF OUR LIFE IS THE FORM OF OUR ART"

THE REQUIREMENTS (all of them) OF OUR LIFE (simply, in many ways it is one and the same life, as the requirements are not plural, but singular, hence) IS (not 'are' there are no plurals here, the Requirements, a monolithic unsorted bundle of demands, formulated for the most part elsewhere, but acceded to blindly, somehow still we manage to make art 'do the work' as we say) THE FORM OF OUR ART.

—*Diane di Prima's articulation of a "poetics"*[111]

"ART IS MAGIC" = another (more masculine?) articulation. Magic to one person often is consciously scavenged, sacrificed, fought and/or killed for by another whose life-force testifies no omission. How? By being availabe. To? "The monolithic unsorted bundle of demands . . ."

Acceding blindly is the secret (the liturgy, if you will). Acceding blindly requires faith, trust, nobility, loyalty. Acceding blindly = bowing to yourself.

Daily doing the ten thousand things is churning one's *chi,* which leaves its stamp on the ten thousand things. Said stamp soon enough signatures the ten-thousand-and-oneth—which for a writer is . . . writing! It can't be helped. Writers write. If you are a writer, eventually (just *because*) the ten thousand things *will* include writing.

Writing isn't something that exists separate from the writer—until it is finished. "Finished" *means* having a life of its own, indeed a legacy, even karma, of its own. Once writing is finished, it drifts off into space and enters the psyche of the beings who cross its path. Before it is finished, it wends its way through *your* anguish, guilt, greed, hate, and delusion.

AND through *your* joy, grace, bliss. Nursing the baby, ironing the shirt, tossing a salad, paying a bill—being available to one's self by these means—means the same thing as writing. They show up in your writing because you show up in them and they become you.

PROCESS = UNIFYING PRINCIPLE. It doesn't matter what you are or how you go about being/becoming it. It doesn't even matter if anyone understands. For a writer, however, it very much matters that your work derives from a UNIFYING PRINCIPLE—your own personal esthetic confluence of internal and external.

"To personalize the rainpipe," painter Edward Hopper summarized, seeking an esthetic confluence of internal and external. "The way in which a few objects are arranged on a table, or a curtain billows in the breeze can set the mood and indicate the kind of person who inhabits the room."[112]

What we are about artistically is subtle—as is how we go about being/becoming "it." Hopper required lengthy periods of gestation. (Very little of his actual time was spent painting.)

James Joyce, meanwhile, worked anywhere, everywhere, carting his voluminous notes, revisions, little scraps of paper and reference books around in a valise.

Right in the midst of all their activity [read: extended family cooking Christmas dinner] in the kitchen sat Joyce. He liked to work there, where the light was best, and would sit there reading, with his feet propped up on the table, or writing, with his papers spread across it. Their chatter never bothered him.[113]

In the Proteus episode of *Ulysses* Stephen Dedalus ponders the difference between audible art (music, literature) in which symbols follow one another—flow through time—and visible art (painting, sculpture) in which symbols appear all at once—outside time. Stephen distinguishes the two as *nacheinander* (one after the other—the audible) and *nebeneinander* (next to each other—the visible). *Finnegans Wake,* beyond time, history, beginning, ending, is Joyce's writerly solution. The question itself—his "unifying principle."

That is, the person who would have left a friend hanging who had done her a favor, also wouldn't have stuck through thick and thin to the business of making poems. It is the same discipline throughout—what Pound called "a 'man' [read 'woman'] standing by [her] Word."

—*Diane di Prima*[114]

An "Artist-First" lives with an inexorable bundle of soul purposes. One of them is BEAUTY. "For us, who had replaced religion, family, society, ethics with Beauty, who saw ourselves as in the service of Beauty, no warnings were understood, no traps anticipated. To go down, in the service of That—that was the ultimate grace," asserts poet Diane di Prima.[115]

While various cultures in various periods have upheld BEAUTY as the ultimate moral standard (e.g., the

Heian period in Japan), for an "Artist-First," the Heian period is NOW. Rare is the time when a standard other than an aesthetic one would supersede an aesthetic one. Or at least not exclude the aesthetic one from first tier considerations. BEAUTY IS TRUTH. It's *that* simple (for an "Artist-First").

Or let's say it's simple if it's in your blood. (For an "Artist-First," it's a no-brainer.) But if it's not—if you question, wonder—"Is it so?" or "Does it *have* to be so? or Worth the effort/sacrifice?"—behind your question is the assumption that it is. This leads to preoccupation with the "eight worldly concerns": gain/loss, pleasure/pain, praise/blame, fame/obscurity. These eight thoughts cloud an artist's mind. (Distract her.)

TRUTH (*and* BEAUTY) run deep. Their well is impermeable.

The truth is that all artists are "Artists-First." (There is no other kind.) One, however, doesn't choose to be an artist. One recognizes that one already is. One hears herself, sees what belongs to her and claims it.

It was the same organ of recognition that is at work when one's whole being says "yes" to a painting, a piece of music, even though it is like nothing we've known before, even though it takes an incredible stretch to stay with it, to actually *hear* it, or see it. There is some infallible mechanism in us, something like a dowsing rod of the heart, and it moves in us sometimes—moves seldom, but with total authority.

—*Diane di Prima*[116]

" 'Chance,' James Joyce once said, 'furnishes me what I need. I am like a man who stumbles along; my foot strikes something, I bend over and it is exactly what I want.' "[117] This is the Joyce who myopically picked from a crowd the woman essential to his writing—the same who said "I have all the words . . . What I am seeking is the perfect order of the words in the sentence."[118]

To those who protested that Joyce's work was not in English, Samuel Beckett admonished:

You cannot complain that this stuff is not written in English. It is not written at all. It is not to be read . . . It is to be looked at and listened to. His writing is not about something. It is that something itself.[119]

When Diane di Prima first read Paracelsus she never dreamed that he would change her way of seeing the world forever. While she read, there was a part of her that simply recognized even the most obscure portions as "inevitable and *true.*" She wasn't even sure what alchemy meant, but she *knew* absolutely that it would (from then on) be a part of her life.

When Chardin decided to paint rabbit fur, he had never painted fur before. He *knew* he shouldn't try it hair by hair:

Here is an object which I must aim to reproduce . . . In order to concentrate my mind on reproducing it faithfully, I must forget everything I have seen, even including the manner in which such objects have ben handled by others. I must place it at such a distance that I cannot see the details. I must work at representing the gen-

eral mass as accurately as possible, the shades and col-
ors, the contours, the effects of light and shade.

John Updike comments "His [Chardin's] rabbit fur explodes in flurries of dry brushstrokes; the limpness of death erases anatomy and almost returns these fruits of the hunt to the mottled background of stone. Rabbit fur taught Chardin a certain atmospheric mistiness that carried over into his depictions of fruit. His peaches and plums look furry, whereas the cats with which he decorated his early, larger still lifes do not."[120]

For Joyce, di Prima, Chardin, Beckett, Updike— "Artists-First"—their hearts are their "dowsing rod." "Yes!" is the answer that dips over gold. It's a law of the "Artist-First" Universe.

The ubiquitous moon, its transparent light, defines a space where nothing leaves a trace. Indeed, to gaze at the moon is to liberate oneself from the pain of remembrance, from the futility of trying to recapture what is ineluctably gone.

Autumn leaves are beautiful partly because in a month, the tree's limbs will be bare. Spring blossoms are breathtaking partly because a month before, the same branch jutted awkwardly into the stormy ether. Implicit in the branch are all four seasons. Nostalgia is for our own ever-evolving nature.

Just as Cezanne had to paint differently to prove that he saw differently, we have to write differently to effect our different understanding.

For example, a Tibetan *thangka* painter's task is to draw a god to precise centuries-old specifications. Is this "art" or is it simply a painstaking imitation?

The answer depends on the quality of the attention of the draftsperson.

For some *thangka* painters, the world reduces itself to the deity during the time of painting—the deity paints the deity. The painter's brush is merely the instrument through which this feat is accomplished. His skill has not so much to do with painting as with listening. Hearing himself, the world and the deity, he hears the Way to paint the deity. The painter who produces a mere likeness is someone who allows the subtle voice of the deity to slip by unnoticed.

The sound that issues from the striking of emptiness is an endless and wondrous voice that resounds before and after the fall of the hammer.

Dogen, Bendowa

While the subtle voice of a deity can sound like silence, an "Artist-First" (knowing that every silence is unique), susses out *this* silence's original nature.

Sometimes we need to hear an outer sound in order to tap into an inner one. Lapping waves, crickets, birds—their vectors and tensors—qualify silence.

A FELLOW MAGE

———

A word score can be anything. You are the composer. Compose a score of words.

Endow small modular structures with comedy, tragedy, rhyme. Choreograph a solstice, an opera, a charade. Set a choral piece. Dedicate a shrine. Jigsaw the gestures of one who speaks in sign.

Include or not—stage directions, asides, contextual/historical information—or *make the whole thing* a stage direction, aside, contextual/historical information.

Your play "Packing," for example, might have four parts (groups of people who pack and talk). Light a stick of incense. Use its flame to parse your gloss on human foibles.

A MAGIC PALIMPSEST

———

"Woodthrushes were caroling from the chartreuse hardwood"

"hundreds of fireflies flashing their green lanterns over the high grass"

"the ethereal crepuscular sky"

"kites hovered in the warm air, piercing the murmur of village life with their thin, clear cries"

Take up a slate. Wipe it clean. Write up, down, zigzag, slanted. Make shapes and smells and noises with your words. Color each letter, or syllable or sound. Wipe *it* clean. (Decide beforehand how long you'll go.)

GLASSINE ENVELOPES

[exercise]

———

A generation ago, poets played by writing lines for fortune cookies. Which is not about telling fortunes. It's about flexing one's perspicacity.

Write 'em down on little strips. Roll 'em up. Tie 'em shut. Later you can determine *their* fortune (decide what you want to do with them).

WILD GOOSE

———

Each of us has a divine name. Each time we "wrestle with God" our divine name is up for reconsideration. Writers (whose weapons are "directed compassion," softening awareness, simply allowing) naturally want to stay current,

Some say that our divine name represents the thing about ourselves that we hate the most (because it is the quality that most uniquely shapes our life). The thing that we struggle with hardest is also the thing with which we spend the most time, to which we most open ourselves, in the face of which we most change (to ease the pain). The resulting transformation of consciousness (reflected in personal presence, luminosity, shimmering light, dazzling "suchness") calls for a new name, a new sound denoting one's more inclusive (authentic) way of resonating with the world.

Facing a blank page/screen writers wrestle with God daily. Their words are powerful and mysterious. "Who

am I to struggle so boldly?" "Who invited me to fight?"
"How can language be such a life and death battle?"

Listen to John Updike:

*In her full-bosomed sweet voice Stella was saying
"Then we add two level teaspoons of dry mustard—
now, pay attention, Mavie, and watch how I scrape it
level with the knife—and just a* splash, *half a teacup
you could say but I never measure, of the dry bread-
crumbs we pounded fine, to give the basting body, and
then we add the moistener, you can use most anything
but spit, my Aunt Dorothea used to say—she was a
character, dear old Aunt Dode, all bent over like a
comma. You can use drippings from the ham, or prune
juice, or my daddy down home used to favor a shot-
glass of elderberry wine"—pronounced* waahn—"*but
Mr. Wilmot with his tender tummy likes his cider vine-
gar, so here goes three tablespoons: one, two, three like
that."* That *became two syllables,* tha-yit; *he could men-
tally see Stella's chins doubling as she looked down lovingly into her task. "Now I'm going to let you stir a
minute while I see how you trimmed the fat. I declare,
I think you cut too deep, Mavie. You're meant just to
slice away the rind, all but a collar around the shank
bone here, and leave all the good fat you can—it has*

*another hour in the oven to go, and we don't want it all
dried out, now do we, little sweet-heart?"*[121]

"My goodness, Mavie," he [Reverend Clarence
Arthur Wilmot, having just awakened to the fact that
There is no God] overhears, "don't be so stingy with the
brown sugar—we Americans like our ham *sweet.*" His
wife's bossy babble to the little Irish girl, patronizing,
parochial, ignorant (of her vanity and bigotry) and
painfully (the rift between them now that he "knows" is
unbridgeable) unaware of Wilmot's newfound truth:
There is no God. ("Clarence could not hear Mavie's mur-
mured, chastened reply" Updike omnipotently tells us,
but it's a moot point. In Mavie's case, not-hearing is the
same as hearing.)

Here, in a paragraph, is a portrait of Stella (her self-
righteous unconsciousness). How is her name precisely
correct?

Portrait your own paragraph and name it (like a
painter *names* a painting).

If you are a novelist (or simply interested in character
development), try writing a second description of the
same person after a period of growth. What is her name
now?

MULTIDIMENSIONALITY
AS STYLE

[exercise]

———

Quiet yourself and allow your mind to drift backward in time to a moment when you were feeling passionately. Whether the feeling was grief, sorrow, regret, sadness, loss, or abandonment doesn't matter so much as the intensity with which you experienced it.

Record the moment from three different perspectives.

Begin by sinking deeply into the full spectrum of the event. Scrub its periphery, dirty corners, and underbelly for information that may have escaped you at the time. Do someone's words still ring with clarity? As you record them, capture their particular inflection or dialect. Was it overcast or raining, brilliantly sunny or just beginning to grow dark? Suggest the season, the lighting, and the time of day without necessarily stating them. Suggest the geographic location or possibly feature certain aspects of it as it calibrated your emotion.

Repeat this exercise from the viewpoint of two other sentient beings. One could be human—someone actually present at the time or present in your recollected imagination. Or it could be someone that you wish had been present.

The second could be non-human—an animal, pet, doll, angel, mythical being—or it could be a plant, stone, mountain, or stream. It could be a tree that overheard the whole story. It could be a child that happened to pass and surmised (illogically like a child) the bull's-eye essence of the situation.

The point of the three stories is to layer your experience with a multidimensionality of perspective (and therefore meaning).

[exercise]

———————

[An outdoor setting is recommended but not mandatory for this exercise.]

Concentrate on hearing something that you've never heard before. Even if you are in nature, your never-before-heard sound may or may not be natural. A natural setting, however, helps open you to yourself.

You may hear soft scurrying of an unidentified animal, the subtle shifting of a dune's edgy crust, rain before it falls, as it readies itself. Or you may hear your heart admitting an impossible-to-imagine love, your soul yearning for God (the fierceness of it), your willingness, finally, to release your cancer-stricken mother. You might hear your daughter vie for guidance (the undercurrent of her need and her abashedness), the depth of your husband's exhaustion, the extremity of your own ordinarily screened-out fatigue.

Allow the sounds to mill around, drift a bit, transform

into other sounds as they float through your conscious-ness, nourishing you with the power, freedom, shock, or relief of their oddments of truth.

As you work, free associate to your own vocabulary. Interrupt yourself, digress, and indulge in off-the-wall spontaneous commentary.

Don't make sense. Please no one—as you penetrate, perhaps, a part of yourself that frightens you. If you look carefully, you may find that what keeps you from yourself (from making friends with yourself) is some old, unexamined belief held by one whose judgment you have long since failed to take seriously. Yet the threat of that person's rejection is still alive—a disapproval obstructing intimacy with the one person who truly can make you happy.

BURST SILENCE WITH SILENCE

[exercise]

———

Racing concerned everyone. During the whole month of August my mother would close down her dancing school and go to the races. So would my grandmother, Lalla. Her figure at the races is ingrained in several people's memories: a large hat at a rakish angle that she wore with no consideration for anyone behind her, one hand on her hip, one hand on her hat, and a blue jacaranda blossom pinned to the shoulder of her dusty black dress, looking off into the drama of the one-hundred-yard stretch with the intensity of one preparing for the coming of the Magi. When the races were over, groups would depart for dinner, dance till early morning, go swimming and have a breakfast at the Mount Lavinia Hotel. Then to bed till noon when it was time for the races once more. The culmination of the season was the Governor's Cup stakes. Even during the war the August races were not to be postponed.

Ceylon could have been invaded during the late after-noon as most of the Light Infantry was at the race track during these hours.[122]

Convey the unconveyable. Say what can't be said. Be so specific that you leave out the main point. Be exacting about the unpindownable, the never-quite-articulated, the *unhearable* river pulsing beneath an icy crust ready to burst with silence.

LISTENING IS FOREVER:
AN APOTHEOSIS

Our way should be like that of a bird or a fish. We should pass through our environment without a trace of our activity, leaving the earth and the mind undisturbed. Our way is to walk like Buddha. Buddha's footsteps leave no trace, no sound, no mark. When we walk with Buddha's footsteps, we do not disturb anyone or anything with our bodies, speech, or minds.

—*Les Kaye*[123]

BUJI LISTENING

Seeing forms with the whole body and mind, hearing
sounds with the whole body and mind, one understands
them intimately.

—*Zen Master Dogen*[124]

"Intimately" means not knowing. Knowing implies you
and the thing known. Not knowing just is.

No one can give us listening. But when listening happens, others can acknowledge it because they have been
included. One must already be listening before one can
receive listening.

The imagining ear *is* listening. (Without listening
there is no imagining ear.) *Buji* listening is listening from
the sidelines.

Once we are aware of listening, we become aware of
moments when we break listening. When we break listening, we simply acknowledge it and return to listening. Ac-
knowledging an action, taking full responsibility for it,
making it one's own (thereby becoming intimate with it)

empowers one to free oneself from the consequences of one's action.

Gradually we become so one with listening that listening isn't breakable.

Listening is soft. A sound occurs and you cradle it, gently.

Listening is harmonic. Being in tune, you hear the whole chord, not just the melodic line.

Listening is playful. A hodge-podge of sublime, voodoo, spooky, exotic, weird.

Listening is virtual. Wrapped in a spell, you experience the spell, sometimes more powerfully than your actual life.

Listening is subtle. You can skimp on depth, but your connection with the speaker will be negatively affected.

Listening is yielding. "Bend an ear" means your whole listening nature.

Listening is rhythmical. You catch the beat of the other person's essence and modulate (dum-tee-dum-tee-dum) your interjections accordingly.

Listening is multi-tasked. Simultaneously, the listener receives, organizes, makes meaning, responds, and processes the feelings that arise in herself.

Listening is generous. You give, first yourself, then the speaker, your entire attention.

Listening is willing. There is a word for people who only hear what is already in their heads.

Listening is setting aside your defenses (for the time being). Upholding defenses requires psychic energy that, if you are listening, rightfully belongs to the other person.

Listening is personal, therefore creative. A jazz musician hunched over his keyboard is listening to himself, wherein the next note resides.

Listening is forever. Not only does everything we do reverberate for eternity. *How* we do anything reverberates for eternity. *How* we do anything is forever.

Listening isn't just listening. Listening is the meeting point of souls.

Another person gathers together a small piece of her consciousness and entrusts it to the care of your consciousness. *How* you treat it means everything.

Anything less than exquisite listening weakens our evolutionary development.

Words are forever. When we say them, their effect lasts forever. When we hear them, their effect lasts forever.

NOTES

1. Pine, *The Zen Works of Stonehouse: Poems and Talks of a Fourteenth Century Chinese Hermit*
2. Remen, *My Grandfather's Blessings: Stories of Strength, Refuge, and Belonging*, p.49
3. Trungpa, *Dharma Art*
4. Matthiessen, *Tigers in the Snow*, p. 71
5. Cather, *My Antonia*, p. 108
6. Garafola and Foner, *Dance for a City: Fifty Years of the New York Ballet*, p. 120
7. ibid., p. 74
8. Berry, *Harlan Hubbard: Life and Work*, p. 68
9. ibid.
10. ibid., p. 70: "How far he was from success in the art world is shown by his sale of a commissioned 'river scene' to Hanover College in 1966—after working nearly half a century as an artist—for $175, the highest price he had ever received for a painting. How thoroughly he disregarded the possibility of success in the art world is shown by his long detachment from his own early work. The paintings he made between 1920 and 1940 were stored in his old studio in Fort Thomas, evidently at the beginning of the shanty boat life in 1944, and he did not look at them again for nearly thirty years."
11. Marcus, *Dear Genius: The Letters of Ursula Nordstrom*, p. xxvii
12. Lew, *One God Clapping: The Spiritual Path of a Zen Rabbi*, p. 245

13. Huang T'ing-chien (1045–1105), an outstanding poet of the Sung dynasty, was especially admired in Japan by Zen monks. T'ao Yuan-ming (365–427) is noted for his simple but deeply philosophical depictions of rural life.

14. Batchelor, "Nagarjuna's *Verses from the Center,*" *Tricycle,* Issue 38, Winter 2000, p. 30

15. Ashworth, *Once in a House on Fire,* p. 51

16. ibid.

17. ibid.

18. Spurling, *The Unknown Matisse: A Life of Henri Matisse: The Early Years, 1869–1908,* p. 361

19. Koren, *Wabi-Sabi for Artists, Designers, Poets, and Philosophers,* p. 42

20. Parini, *Robert Frost: A Life,* p. 388

21. Lew, *One God Clapping: The Spiritual Path of a Zen Rabbi,* p. 282

22. Ibid., p. 291

23. Pissarro, *Camille Pissarro,* p. 183

24. Ibid.

25. Beer, "Art Making the Artist: An Interview with Robert Beer," *Tricycle,* Issue 33, Fall 1999

26. di Prima, *Recollections of my Life as a Woman,* p. 156–157

27. Lopez, *Arctic Dreams: Imagination and Desire in a Northern Landscape,* p. 410

28. Parini, *Robert Frost: A Life,* p. 174

29. Bernier, *Matisse, Picasso, Miro as I Knew Them,* p. 30

30. Parini, *Robert Frost: A Life,* p. 214

31. Spring, *Fairfield Porter: A Life in Art,* p. 262

32. Garafola and Foner, *Dance for a City: Fifty Years of the New York Ballet,* p. 128

33. ibid., p. 125

34. ibid., p. 132

35. Lieber, *Willem de Kooning: Reflections in the Studio,* p. 17

36. ibid., p. 30

37. ibid., p. 50

38. ibid., p. 50

39. Asayesh, *Saffron Sky: A Life between Iran and America,* p. 213

40. ibid., p. 16

41. Spring, *Fairfield Porter: A Life in Art,* p. 174

42. ibid., p. 62

43. ibid., p. 174

44. Anderson, *Being Upright: Zen Meditation and the Bodhisattva Precepts,* p. 81

45. Asayesh, *Saffron Sky: A Life between Iran and America,* p. 16.

46. Leaska, *Granite and Rainbow: The Hidden Life of Virginia Woolf,* p. 212

47. Pissarro, *Camille Pissarro,* p. 215

48. Quoted in "Dharma in the Republic of Desire," *Tricycle,* Issue 33, Fall 1999, p. 116

49. Ramirez-Christensen, *Heart's Flower: The Life and Poetry of Shinkei,* p. 192

50. ibid., p. 191

51. Pissarro, *Camille Pissarro,* p. 91

52. Chadwick, *Crooked Cucumber: The Life and Zen Teaching of Shunryu Suzuki,* p. 351

53. Pissarro, *Camille Pissarro,* p. 165

54. Berry, *Harlan Hubbard: Life and Work,* p. 66

55. ibid., p. 60

56. ibid., p. 53

57. Pissarro, *Camille Pissarro,* p. 143

58. ibid., p. 272

59. di Prima, *Recollections of My Life as a Woman,* p. 156

60. Pissarro, *Camille Pissarro,* p. 257

61. Lew, *One God Clapping: The Spiritual Path of a Zen Rabbi,* p. 167

62. Cokinos, *Hope Is a Thing with Feathers: A Personal Chronicle of Vanished Birds,* p. 163

63. ibid., p. 61–62

64. ibid., p. 126–127

65. ibid., p. 127–128

66. di Prima, *Recollections of My Life as a Woman*, p. 222

67. Leaska, *Granite and Rainbow: The Hidden Life of Virginia Woolf*, p. 12

68. Lew, *One God Clapping: The Spiritual Path of a Zen Rabbi*, p. 261

69. Riding, "Arts Abroad," *The New York Times*, p. 210

70. Lew, *One God Clapping: The Spiritual Path of a Zen Rabbi*, p. 210

71. ibid., p. 210

72. ibid., p. 154

73. ibid., p. 321

74. Thurman and Wise, *Circling the Sacred Mountain: A Spiritual Adventure through the Himalayas*, p. 17

75. Aitken, *The Practice of Perfection*

76. Kaye, *Zen at Work*, p. 162

77. Nabokov "declared one evening, to be challenged by Véra, in a modulated, musical voice, 'And Coleridge?'" from Schiff, *Véra (Mrs. Vladimir Nabokov)*, p. 276

78. Norris in Thorpe, *Work and the Life of the Spirit*, p. 230

79. Loori, *The Eight Gates of Zen: Spiritual Training in an American Zen Monastery*, p. 111–112

80. ibid., p. 121

81. Parini, *Robert Frost: A Life*, p. 386

82. ibid., p. 194

83. ibid., p. 166

84. ibid.

85. ibid., p. 164

86. Joyce, *Dubliners*, p. 182

87. Amarasekera, *Ceylon Sunday Times*, 29.1.78. [from Ondaatje, *Running in the Family*, p. 1]

88. Ondaatje, *Running in the Family*, p. 17

89. Leaska, *Granite and Rainbow: The Hidden Life of Virginia Woolf*, p. 14
90. Ramirez-Christensen, *Heart's Flower: The Life and Poetry of Shinkei*, p. 194
91. ibid.
92. Karl, *George Eliot: Voice of a Century*, p. 75–76
93. Crane, *Bones of the Master: A Buddhist Monk's Search for the Lost Heart of China*, p. 225
94. di Prima, *Recollections of My Life as a Woman*, p. 148
95. Loori, *The Eight Gates of Zen: Spiritual Training in an American Zen Monastery*, p. 183
96. di Prima, *Recollections of My Life as a Woman*, p. 136
97. Thorpe, *Work and the Life of the Spirit*, p. 208
98. Crane, *Bones of the Master: A Buddhist Monk's Search for the Lost Heart of China*, p. 261
99. ibid., p. 270
100. ibid., p. 25
101. Garafola, *Dance for a City: Fifty Years of the New York City Ballet*, p. 166
102. Parini, *Robert Frost: A Life*, p. 333
103. ibid., p. 281
104. ibid., p. 198
105. Ableman, *On Good Land: The Autobiography of an Urban Farm*, p. 25
106. ibid.
107. Parini, *Robert Frost: A Life*, p. 342
108. Thurman and Wise, *Circling the Sacred Mountain: A Spiritual Adventure through the Himalayas*, p. 271
109. Breashears, *High Exposure: An Enduring Passion for Everest and Unforgiving Places*, p. 92
110. di Prima, *Recollections of My Life as a Woman*, p. 224
111. ibid., p. 226–227
112. Levin, *Edward Hopper: An Intimate Biography*, p. 219
113. Maddox, *Nora: The Real Life Molly Bloom*, p. 110

114. di Prima, *Recollections of My Life as a Woman,* p. 202
115. ibid., p. 369
116. ibid., p. 422–423
117. Maddox, *Nora: The Real Life Molly Bloom,* p. 23
118. ibid., p. 158
119. ibid., p. 252
120. Updike, *New York Times Review,* p. 8
121. Updike, *In the Beauty of the Lilies,* p. 86
122. Ondaatje, *Running in the Family,* p. 49
123. Kaye, *Zen at Work,* p. 163
124. Tanahashi, *Enlightenment Unfolds: The Essential Teachings of Zen Master Dogen*

BIBLIOGRAPHY

Ableman, Michael. *On Good Land: The Autobiography of an Urban Farm.* Chronicle Books: San Francisco, 1998.

Aitken, Robert. *The Practice of Perfection.* Pantheon Books: New York, 1994.

Anderson, Reb. *Being Upright: Zen Meditation and the Bodhisattva Precepts.* Rodmell Press: Berkeley, 2001.

Asayesh, Gelareh. *Saffron Sky: A Life between Iran and America.* Beacon Press: Boston, 1999.

Ashworth, Andrea. *Once in a House on Fire.* Henry Holt and Company: New York, 1998.

Batchelor, Stephen. "Nagarjuna's *Verses from the Center.*" *Tricycle: The Buddhist Review.* Spring 2000, p. 25–30.

Beer, Robert. "Art Making the Artist: An Interview with Robert Beer." *Tricycle: The Buddhist Review.* Fall 1999, p. 4–59

———. "Dharma in the Republic of Desire," *Tricycle: The Buddhist Review.* Fall 1999, p. 69–116.

Bernier, Rosamond. *Matisse, Picasso, Miro As I Knew Them.* Alfred A. Knopf: New York, 1991.

Berry, Wendell. *Harlan Hubbard: Life and Work.* The University Press of Kentucky: Lexington, 1990.

Breashears, David. *High Exposure: An Enduring Passion for Everest and Unforgiving Places.* Simon & Schuster: New York, 1990.

Cather, Willa. *My Antonia.* Penguin Classics: New York, 1914.

Chadwick, David. *Crooked Cucumber: The Life and Zen Teaching of Shunryu Suzuki.* Broadway: New York, 1999.

Cokinos, Christopher. *Hope Is a Thing with Feathers: A Personal Chronicle of Vanished Birds.* Jeremy P. Tarcher: A Member of Penguin Putnam: New York, 2000.

Crane, George. *Bones of the Master: A Buddhist Monk's Search for the Lost Heart of China.* A Living Planet Book, Bantam Books: New York, 2000.

di Prima, Diane. *Recollections of My Life as a Woman.* Viking: New York, 2001.

Garafola, Lynn and Foner, Eric. *Dance for a City: Fity Years of the New York City Ballet.* Columbia University Press: New York, 1999.

Joyce, James. *Dubliners.* Bantam: New York, 1914.

Karl, Frederick R. *George Eliot: Voice of a Century.* W. W. Norton & Company: New York, 1995.

Kaye, Les. *Zen at Work.* Three Rivers Press: New York, 1996.

Koren, Leonard. *Wabi-Sabi for Artists, Designers, Poets, and Philosophers.* Stone Bridge Press: Berkeley, 1994.

Leaska, Mitchell. *Granite and Rainbow: The Hidden Life of Virginia Woolf.* Farrar Straus Giroux: New York, 1998.

Levin, Gail. *Edward Hopper: An Intimate Biography.* Alfred Knopf: New York, 1996.

Lew, Alan. *One God Clapping: The Spiritual Path of a Zen Rabbi.* Kodansha International: New York, 1999.

Lieber, Edvard. *Willem de Kooning: Reflections in the Studio.* Harry N. Abrams, Inc. Publishers: New York, 2000.

Loori, John Daido. *The Eight Gates of Zen: Spiritual Training in an American Zen Monastery.* Dharma Communications: Mt. Tremper, 1992.

Lopez, Barry. *Arctic Dreams: Imagination and Desire in a Nothern Landscape.* Charles A. Scribner: New York, 1986.

Maddox, Brenda. *Nora: The Real Life Molly Bloom.* Houghton Mifflin: Boston, 1988.

Marcus, Leonard S., ed. *Dear Genius: The Letters of Ursula Nordstrom.* HarperCollins Publishers: New York, 1998.

Matthiessen, Peter. *Tigers in the Snow.* North Point Press: San Francisco, 2000.

Ondaatje, Michael. *Running in the Family.* Vintage Books, A Division of Random House, Inc.: New York, 1993.

Parini, Jay. *Robert Frost: A Life.* Henry Holt and Company: New York, 1999.

Pine, Red. *The Zen Works of Stonehouse: Poems and Talks of a Fourteenth Century Chinese Hermit.* Translated by Red Pine Mercury House: San Francisco, 1999.

Pissarro, Joachim. *Camille Pissarro.* Harry N. Abrams, Inc. Publishers: New York, 1993.

Proust, Marcel. *In Search of Lost Time.* The Modern Library: New York, 1998.

Ramirez-Christensen, Esperanza. *Heart's Flower: The Life and Poetry of Shinkei.* Stanford University Press: Stanford, 1994.

Remen, Rachel Naomi. *My Grandfather's Blessings: Stories of Strength, Refuge, and Belonging.* Riverhead Books, A Member of Penguin Putnam: New York, 2000.

Riding, Alan. "Arts Abroad," *The New York Times,* June 5, 2001.

Schiff, Stacy. *Véra (Mrs. Vladimir Nabokov).* The Modern Library: New York: 1999.

Spring, Justin. *Fairfield Porter: A Life in Art.* Yale University Press: New Haven, 2000.

Spurling, Hilary. *The Unknown Matisse: A Life of Henri Matisse: The Early Years, 1869–1908.* Alfred A. Knopf: New York, 1998.

Suzuki, Shunryu. *Zen Mind, Beginner's Mind.* Shambhala: Boston, 1970.

Tanahashi, Kazuaki, ed. *Enlightenment Unfolds: The Essential Teachings of Zen Master Dogen.* Shambala: Boston, 1999.

Thorpe, Douglas, ed. *Work and the Life of the Spirit.* Mercury House: San Francisco, 1998.

Thurman, Robert and Wise, Tad. *Circling the Sacred Mountain: A Spiritual Adventure through the Himalayas.* Bantam Books: New York, 1999.

Trungpa, Chogyam. *Dharma Art.* Shambhala: Boston & London: 1996.

Updike, John. *In the Beauty of the Lilies.* Fawcett Columbine: New York, 1996.

Updike, John. "Chardin." *The New York Review,* August 10, 2000.